MIKE THRUSSELL
The Tactical Shore Angler

Peridot Press

First published in 2017 by Peridot Press Ltd
12 Deben Mill Business Centre, Melton, Woodbridge, Suffolk IP12 1BL

ISBN: 978-1-911382-18-8

Set and designed by Theoria Design
www.theoriadesign.com

Contents

'Mike Thrussell's latest book is one of the very best 'how-to' publications I have ever read and THE best on shore fishing. It explains where, when and why... and then how, the perfect chronological order. Blimey, it even explains the weather! It's well written and very well produced and whether you have never cast a pulley rig - or even don't know what it is or how it works - or if you are a regular at your local pier, beach or estuary I guarantee that your fishing (sorry: angling) will be all the better for reading it.'
    Keith Arthur, presenter, *Tight Lines*

'If you are serious about your sea angling, you seriously need to read this book! Positively packed full of practical pointers, I challenge anyone to not learn a great deal from *The Tactical Shore Angler*, a title set to fast become a go-to reference for budding and experienced shore anglers alike.'
    Bill Brazier, Editor/Founder, *Off the Scale* magazine

'Mike Thrussell's latest book is a unique and masterful work, which is based on a lifetime's experience with rod and line. Mike's meticulous note making after every expedition, even on fishless days, has ensured that the reader will glean many nuggets of wisdom from one of Europe's foremost anglers. For many of us lesser mortals *The Tactical Shore Angler* will become a regular go-to bible, one which is destined to become a modern day classic.'
    Norman Dunlop, former National Sea Angling Adviser, Irish Central Fisheries Board

'Mike Thrussell is arguably the most respected angler on our shores today. This book is a comprehensive guide to tactics and techniques that will bring success on the many and varied marks around the UK coastline. Essential reading for shore anglers of all abilities, it goes beyond the 'how' and explains the 'why'.'
    Paul Dennis, Editor, *Total Sea Fishing* magazine

'A wealth of angling experience is packed into the pages of Mike Thrussell's book – with everything from types of fishing venue, bait and plenty of rigs. It will be a great reference point for all.'
    Cliff Brown, Editor, *Sea Angler* magazine

Introduction

Dictionaries describe angling as a 'sport' or 'pastime' of fishing with a rod and line. The word 'fishing', in its own right, is described much the same. Yet the two words could not be further removed.

To me, fishing is what it suggests. It means to fish, just to fish, nothing more. There are those that are happy just fishing. In fact, many describe themselves as fishermen, merely happy to be by the sea shore listening to the rhythmical song of the surf, the cry of the seagulls, watching a summer's dawn break over the horizon, or eyeing a winter's sun melt in to a calm sea as another day passes. Often you hear the words, "I'm just happy to be out and about in the fresh air for some peace and quiet, and I don't care if I don't catch!" Really?

Ask yourself this: if you caught nothing over the duration of several fishing trips, how long would your enthusiasm for fishing last? It's been proven: not long at all! It's human nature to want a reward for time spent. Fishing is no different!

'Angling', as a word, is much more descriptive, and has a far deeper meaning. It suggests the use of rod and line with a deeper understanding of catching fish. This is an important difference that defines the gap between a fisherman and an angler.

The fisherman goes fishing with no real conviction. He is initially happy to let nature take its course and Lady Luck put the fish on the hook for him with little thought as to how he himself might improve his own catches. Invariably, when Lady Luck deserts him – and she can be fickle and quick to lose her patience – he gets deflated and soon loses interest. If you truly are happy just to be by the sea, then be content in that, but you are missing out on a whole plethora of angling opportunities that results in significant lifelong memories and far fewer fishless days.

The true angler goes way beyond this. His intention, on every trip, is to catch fish. It may be a particular species, a specimen fish of a certain size, or sometimes a fish just for the fun of catching it because it fights hard, but he does this with that intention, deliberately devising a specific strategy that decreases the odds against him. Do this over time and the odds keep decreasing as you learn tips, tricks and tactics that actually do put more fish on the beach. In short, life becomes far more interesting!

There is an old but wise saying, a truism, that puts this in to perspective: "10 per cent of the anglers catch 90 per cent of the fish". Many may not like to be categorised so, some doubt the saying is true; but it is true, and wholly fact! Only you as an individual can decide if you're happy fishing or angling.

The step from fishing to angling is not difficult. It does require some work, as so much in life does, but the rewards are great, and a whole new world is quick to open up. One that gives much greater gratification than simple fishing ever will.

This book is about learning relatively simple tactics that can transform the way you fish, but also dramatically increase your day-to-day catches. These things did not come easily to me either. I had to put the time and effort in to learning this with little help, at least initially, from anyone else. I had to learn from my mistakes.

Much of what I will write has come from a driving passion to catch fish. I am not competitive with other people. Truly, I'm not! I find it combative and far too personal. It is not something I personally enjoy. My adversary is the fish. It is they I want to overcome, not a friend, or other anglers fishing near me. The skill is not in out-fishing the other person. The skill is in out-thinking the fish, a wild creature designed to live in a harsh environment where the simple law is kill or be killed. It is not easy to fool a wild fish. They live and experience just like we do, and from that experience they learn and become ever harder to catch.

This is especially so of the bigger fish, and especially specimen and record-sized fish. The harder they are to catch, the more I want to catch them. To catch them I realise I need to learn more about them, collate this information over time, and, as already mentioned, use this building-brick knowledge given to them by the best teacher of all, Mother Nature, to reduce the odds those fish have on their side to avoid me.

This book is about putting together a strategy and tactical plan that will improve your shore fishing and see your overall catches dramatically increase. What's more, this information, for the most part, will never change. Tackle and technology are forever advancing, but the chapters on ground feature will remain fact for millennia. There is no point in having the best tackle if first you cannot find the fish. The latter is a simple sentence, but a true fact of life many fishermen never fully understand throughout a lifetime's fishing. It's my hope and intention, within the forthcoming pages, to show you where the fish are.

Mike Thrussell
June, 2017

Chapter 1:
Fish in Focus

The native American Indian felt that to catch and then eat any fish, fowl or game gave the hunter the ability to become more as one with the creature. To think its thoughts and better anticipate its every move. This is what made a great hunter. To become a successful angler, we need to also learn the nature, instincts and mannerisms of the fish we want to catch. By understanding the basic functions of a fish, it helps us put our minds in to what the fish are doing in that hidden world under the sea.

There is a reason why fish are different shapes. Mother Nature has designed them to undertake specific roles and to capitalise on specific food sources that live amongst defined ground feature. A fish's shape also dictates, to some extent, how predators ambush and attack. In this way nature achieves a balance within herself that keeps the marine world stable. Every food source is used to the maximum, yet never naturally depleted. This is why it's important to understand those basic functions.

BODY SHAPE
If you look closely at the body shape of a fish, it tells you a lot as to how they feed.

Take bass to start. They are a round-bodied fish with a broad tail and large mouth. The body is streamlined for fast manoeuvring, the tail gives

rapid acceleration, and the mouth is big enough to easily engulf prey that could be up to 20 per cent of the size of the attacking bass. The sleek body can sit in a fast tide, or work through heavy surf tables, but is also adept at working through narrow channels between rocks and weed beds when physically hunting prey. The bass is at home grubbing on the seabed for worms, digging crabs out from under stones, but also chasing prey in the mid and surface layers.

Cod are different. They have a very big head and mouth in relation to the body size with a round body shape. These are designed to invert and scoop, or hoover food up off the bottom, but also use that big mouth to suck in small fish such as whiting, pout, poor cod, rockling and even their own kind. Again a big tail gives power to handle turbulent water, and acceleration power to intercept live prey.

A bull huss has a big head, but a fast-tapering body to the tail, also a flat belly shape. This is a bottom-dweller scouring the seabed for food. It is equally happy in amongst weed beds and rocks where it uses its thin shape to hunt between the rocks looking to scare up small wounded fish, crabs and food left over from other predatory attacks.

Conger eels are long, thin-shaped fish. They are 'ambush artists', adept at taking up home in old pipes and wreckage laying on the seabed, or setting up home lying in amongst the rocks and in cracks, or under rock ledges waiting for hapless prey fish like pouting and poor cod to swim past them.

Flatfish, as the name suggests, are flat in shape and tend to sit on the seabed semi-covered in sand and facing in to the oncoming tide with their eyes looking forwards and upwards. This allows them to smell and see both waterborne food items such as broken-off razorfish, worms and small prey fish heading their way, which they then intercept by powering forwards. Flatties, and especially sole, will also invert and push their heads vertically in to sand to dig out food items.

Rays are another species that sit on the seabed, partially covered in sand, facing in to the oncoming current. Their eyes are ever alert as they scan the seabed for passing prey fish and food. When something happens along, they have a short burst of speed powered by their wings and tend to flop over the bait and smother it, moving it towards the mouth as they settle.

The shark-like tope also have a somewhat flattened belly with a slim manoeuvrable body and big, powerful tail. They swim fast across the seabed, often in packs. This is a deliberate ploy to scare and scatter smaller

fish. They then use their lateral line to first detect prey, then chase them down using eyesight, but also smell when taking already-wounded fish. The tope will then grab and impale caught fish in their mouth, or cut through the body of bigger prey, before swallowing it whole.

Wrasse and bream are slim-profiled, oval-shaped fish designed to cut through a fast tide run or wave swell. Their shape gives them greater stability too, plus the slim shape allows them to weave in and out of dense weed beds and rocks, also manoeuvre easily through and over shallow reef ground.

The shape of fish, then, is well worth studying as it gives you a lot of information, not just as to how the fish feed, but also what type of ground they are best designed to feed over. The importance of this will become apparent as we get to the chapters on ground feature.

HOW FISH SEE

The fact is, even in these enlightened times, we do not fully understand exactly what fish see in the form of colours and images. Research has mainly, and somewhat predictably, been conducted on laboratory fish, and much less so on wild fish. Laboratory conditions cannot simulate accurately the varied depth and environment a wild fish inhabits. Also, without doubt, different species working at different depths and in

different environments will have different vision capabilities designed to maximise their identification of specific food sources.

What we do know is that the eyes and retinas of the majority of fish give a focused and relatively clear image with good contrast and, of course, with the ability to detect movement. Indications are, not surprisingly, that a minimum level of light is necessary for a fish to recognise colour, and that some fish can home in on certain colours their eyes are adapted specifically to recognise. This may be to identify, at a glance, important food fish that are a main part of their diet.

Fish living in shallow inshore water will have a greater degree of colour vision. Deep-water fish living in low-light conditions will see grey or black colours best, so white and black give good contrast, but so too does red, as in deep water this will also look black.

Most fish tend to be short-sighted, but are able to see to some degree in coloured water and in low-light conditions. This also tells us that eyesight is most likely to be used in the final phase of an attack by a predatory fish. Predators are usually drawn to, or initially made aware of lures by either the splash as the lure hits the water, or by the vibration and noise caused by the lure's action in the water.

Fish also have a wide zone in which they can see. Each eye can see 180 degrees, so typically front, side, upwards, downwards and even to the rear. This is a protective mechanism that can give early warning of a predatory attack to aid escape, but can also identify prey that may appear from any angle after passing by. They do have one blind spot that is acutely rearwards of the tail fin. This is a dead spot the eye barely reaches, and is maybe part of the reason why fish rarely swim in straight lines for long, but will deviate off course every few seconds, much the same as a fighter pilot does when in combat. Flying or swimming straight for any period of time is courting disaster, making it easier for a predator to attack.

Fish generally have no eyelids. They don't need eyelids because their environment is wholly moist, so the eye is kept lubricated all the time. This does, though, especially in very clear and shallow water, make them more susceptible to high light levels pushing them deeper down in the water column where light passing through is less intense.

Knowing what we know about the eyesight of fish, we can exploit their nature through our choice of lures. By day, in clear water, coloured lures will often work well. A successful lure colour is Chartreuse, which is especially effective for inshore bass, pollack and wrasse in daylight. A combination of white and red also works well. However, at dusk and dawn, when light levels are low, a black or red lure gives a better silhouette against surface light that predatory fish working below find easier to see.

HOW FISH SMELL FOOD

If you look closely, fish have small openings or holes on the upper jaw in front of the eyes. These are nostrils, but called nares. These open up in to a chamber lined with sensory pads or hairs. Some fish can pump water through these nares to detect waterborne scent from food, while others, such as mackerel, constantly swim forwards allowing water to flood through the nares via incoming pressure. When the pads or hairs pick up scent, this sends a signal to the fish's brain which alerts the fish and identifies the food.

Fish in feeding mode tend to sit facing in to, or swim in to, the oncoming tide, letting the current bring scent from food to them when in feeding mode. They are also capable of detecting small amounts of scent at long range and use this as an initial means of locating dead baits, such as fish, worms and crabs. They then swim, sometimes swinging side-to-side if the scent trail is weak, to maintain contact and will directly home in as the scent trail gets stronger closer to the source.

Another tactic that round-shaped fish like bass use is to face into the tide but allow themselves to drop back slowly with it, their head swinging from side to side to cover a wide area while scanning for waterborne scent. This is a tactic they use in deeper estuary channels, in fast currents around bridges, pier supports, under jetties and the downside inclines of sandbanks. Once a scent trail is detected they power forward to locate the food.

THE LATERAL LINE

The lateral line is the most important detection system a fish has. The lateral line runs along the flanks of the fish's head to the tail and is a sensing organ. It is a row of scales that hide underneath a system of fluid-filled canals and special cells that allow the fish to pick up and receive movement and vibration in surrounding water and transmit these vibrations directly to the brain. This is how fish initially become aware of both prey and potential predatory attack. It is also how shoaling fish, such as mackerel, herring and school bass, stay in tight shoals and appear to move as one. They literally 'feel' the presence of the other shoal members through the water.

The lateral line is also used when manoeuvring in amongst feature and structure, such as rocks, pier and jetty supports, and through submerged gutters, weed beds and sandy gullies.

The lateral line is so effective, it is the reason why anglers sometimes catch totally blind, yet fully healthy fish. The loss of their eyes can be made up for by the effectiveness of the lateral line initially identifying

prey by vibration and direction, but then homing the fish in to that prey and guiding the final attack. Their sense of smell also contributes just as it would with a fully visual fish.

FEEDING PATTERNS

Fish do not feed as we do. They do not have set feeding times, as such. Yes, they are stimulated by the tide, and by weather conditions, but are dependent primarily on the availability of food.

At times, food is abundant and their bellies are full, such as when the crabs peel in May and June, and after storms and heavy seas that have washed worms, shellfish and dead fish ashore in the autumn. This is why sometimes, when we take a fish for the table, on gutting it, the belly is full of sandeel, crab, small baitfish, worms and shellfish. There has been a glut of food and the fish has capitalised on it. During these times they can be picky, less interested in certain food items, becoming preoccupied with what is common, and ignoring the rest. The fishing can be difficult for a few days after such gluts until the fish have digested their food.

Fish are also hunters and no hunter kills with every attack. I have spoken to falconers who tell me that birds of prey, such as falcons and hawks, have an average kill ratio of about one in five attempts. Even sharks are not 100 per cent accurate and may also fall into that one-in-five average. Other marine predators are very likely to be the same.

There are also periods when food is scarce and hard to find: typically, in spring, and in areas of light tides, during the smaller neap tides. During such times a fish's belly may be empty, or carrying just one small item. This may be because it has failed to hunt successfully, but also possibly because food is limited at this specific time.

You may have also heard the phrase 'chasing fish'. This basically means anglers listening to recent reports and targeting fish that may have already been caught, or more likely moved on to new ground days ago. It is also a reference to fish having been feeding to excess during a glut. As we see, they stop eating to digest their food and this can take a couple of days or more before they are looking to feed again.

By learning a little of the design features of the fish we target, we become, much like the native American Indian, more in tune with their needs, habits and feeding patterns, and this in turn makes us far better hunters and anglers.

Chapter 2:
The Right Research

Research is the quick and obvious route to identifying marks and areas within your chosen travelling range that are the most likely to produce good bags of fish, or certain types of species you want to catch. You also need to identify areas that, in turn, fish well during spring, summer, autumn and winter, so that your fishing year is logically spread and your catches remain at a fairly consistent level throughout the full 12 months.

To do this, you need to tap in to the local and national media, and there are several ways in which this can be approached. Modern technology allows us much greater scope at the touch of a key, and more up-to-date information than was ever previously available, but we use this alongside more conventional forms of information, such as books.

MAGAZINES

Monthly magazines are always a great source of information. Magazines are designed to be generally timely, so the features you read in a specific month's issue, dealing with venues or areas, will have been chosen to be read either just as the mark is beginning to fish or a month or two in advance of its best fishing. Treat articles as being predictive, time-wise, and you won't go far wrong.

Good articles in most magazines tend to have a set format and will give the seasons throughout the year when the different species arrive, peak, and leave. This is perfect information, as it avoids you fishing dead time when the species you seek are simply not there, or the fishing is slow and not worth the effort. This allows you to pick only those venues that should fish best at a given time and sees you maximise your efforts within the best time periods.

Also look for hints on the weather patterns that fish best at a particular venue. These should be wind directions, which can be critical at most marks, as the right wind direction creates the perfect surf and dislodges food from the sand and rocks, whereas a wind that flattens the sea may well see the fish go off the feed, resulting in low catches.

Is it best by day or night? Generally speaking, it is the night tides on most marks that give the best fishing. However, gleaning information from an article may see you identify a daylight mark which will be invaluable during the summer months when the dark hours are short.

Tides are also extremely important and these, too, should be covered by the writer. Take notice of what they say and only fish the tides suggested. The person putting pen to paper is obliged to write the facts, for if he does not, then his own reputation is at stake. If you choose to ignore the quoted information, and fish at a time and in a way convenient to you, and you struggle to catch fish, then in part it is your own fault as you ignored potentially good advice.

Other information will include which baits work best for selected species at a given mark. Again this saves time and helps massively towards getting results immediately. Also which rigs to use. Rig choice is critical on some venues and having prior knowledge of what to make and to carry can put way more fish in the bag.

It pays to store your magazines permanently, or at least the venue features that appeal to you. If you catalogue them, then it's easy in the future to locate them and reread them as necessary. Over time you build up a detailed library that will prove hugely important over the coming years as you progress and your fishing targets change.

Another thing that magazines do is carry notable fish catches and news. Pay attention to these pages and take note of venues that consistently produce big fish, or fish of a certain species that might interest you. Over time you'll see patterns, such as a certain venue that produces a majority of its big bass in November, or maybe a beach that is good for plaice in May. This information may not always seem useful at the time, but later, if your interests shift, it will already be there and be invaluable, allowing you to look back over time and make a decision on where and when to go with the best chance of success.

BOOKS

Books still play an important part when researching angling matters.

Books you simply cannot manage without are species identification books. Not only do these identify the different species, and more importantly the least likely caught species, but they carry a lot of information about the habitat, food and migration patterns of many of the fish we seek to catch. If you buy one, you're sure to buy more, as each has its own unique reference format. Modern ones tend to have high quality colour photographs too, and this makes identification so much easier.

Books about actual fishing are also vital. These will carry information on all the things we've already discussed, such as habitat, food preferences, movement, distribution, also various methods by which individual fish can be caught, plus tackle and bait. In the beginning these books are part of the learning curve. As your experience grows, you find that the books become less necessary, and, in a fishing sense, you grow out of them as your own knowledge grows.

THE INTERNET

The one thing anglers are not good at is keeping quiet about the fish they catch. Naturally, when you've enjoyed a good catch, you want to tell the world about it. This is where the internet forum boards come in. The good ones are packed with anglers bursting to tell all and sundry about their latest trip. This has become a primary source of information for both fishermen and especially observant anglers.

By accessing a few forum boards, joining in if you want to, you get access to up-to-date information in what is basically real time. Most posts are made almost immediately after an angler returns from a trip, or their post is written within a couple of days of returning home. It's accurate and almost instant information that can save you a lot of time and expense if you take the trouble to use it. What's more it can lead you to better catches, just like the magazines, by indicating good venues, the best times to fish them, the best baits, rigs, weather patterns and much more. What you cannot gauge is the ability of the fisherman writing the report. A good tip is to trace a few of their previous reports back and see how they fish over a set time period. This will give you a good indication of their abilities and eliminate chance catches.

Most forum boards tend to split their forums in to area-related groups, such as Southwest England, South Wales, North Wales and so on. This makes it easy to either just select an individual area that you want to concentrate on, or spread wider and collate information from several areas. Concentrating on one area is logical, but keeping pace with other areas will help you see long term patterns, such as fish migration south to north in the spring.

What the forum boards also allow is the opportunity to ask questions. The anglers willing to post their catches publicly online are also more likely to respond to questions and give good reliable information to the best of their ability. If you wanted to keep things to yourself, you wouldn't post at all. Use this contact option, as again it is a quick route to reducing those odds stacked against you catching. Always take time to consider whether sending a private message to a forum member might get you a more detailed response than if you posted publicly. It often works out that way!

The internet is also a great tool for researching. It will find you general information on venues to fish, rigs, baits and much more, but it's best for researching the species you want to catch. By diligently searching using different search terms, you'll find downloadable scientific papers on many species that offer a much deeper insight in to the lives and habitat of fish that maybe other forms of knowledge cannot. For instance, common fish that are targeted commercially, such as cod, plaice, turbot, sole and haddock, have all been subjected to major scientific research due to their value as a commercial catch and food source. Such papers can be invaluable and give us a far deeper insight in to habits, habitat and preferred food, than most other information sources!

Facebook is much like the forum boards. Anglers cannot resist posting their catches. They are, though, less likely to divulge the marks they fish than they are on the angling forums. However, it always pays to keep an eye on Facebook and see what people are posting. Good information is often given away. You just need to be aware that it is not as reliable as the angling forum boards regarding the venues fished. That said, it is easy enough to look where the posters are based, and from that work out a few likely venues any good fish may have come from. Usually, if the venue they fished is close to home, they are less likely to mention exactly where they fished. If they travelled a long way, then they tend to spill the beans and be exact about where they fished.

CONVERSATION

Some of the best information comes from direct conversations you have with other anglers. This may be at an angling club, for instance, joining can give you the opportunity to fish alongside more experienced hands. Often they are more than willing to part with tips and tricks, plus visual instruction is a great way to learn. What's more, they'll have a knowledge of some venues that you can look at and research privately in more detail to see what they offer, and if they fit your plan of what you want to fish for.

Equally, always try to strike up conversations when fishing alongside other anglers. Swapping pleasantries with your fishing neighbour can often lead to useful information such as a recent good bag of fish they caught, or a favourite venue they frequently fish, or a big fish they once caught. Try to extract, subtly, when, where and how they caught it. Often they give this information freely. Make a mental note of it and when you get the chance write it down so that you can use it for further research.

Also be observant and watch other anglers while you are fishing. They may know a small spot that produces more fish than elsewhere, which is why they are fishing there. Note that exact spot by using landmarks. Also try and compare their catches. If they are catching more than you, then you are more than likely doing something wrong. Try to find out what it is by talking to them and visually checking out their rigs and baits.

Another good tip is to watch anglers when they park their car. If they walk straight down to the beach and fish, the chances are that they are looking for the easy life and not willing to walk any distance to a better spot. If a person leaves the car and walks a long way up or down the beach to a specific spot, then take notice, as he, or she, is doing that for what is likely to be a very good reason based on their past good catches.

KEEP A PERSONAL FISHING DIARY

I've left the day-to-day fishing diary to last, because it is the most important source of information you'll ever have. Keeping a diary is hard work, but it will pay you back in extra fish time and time again after just a few years. Its pages will reveal patterns of when fish show at certain places, the wind direction that fishes best at a specific venue, what sea state is best, the best baits, rigs, whether to fish in daylight or darkness, and a thousand and one other things. A diary takes time to build, but it is the foundation of your long term strategy and tactics.

When you write your diary, and this can be hand written in book form, or inside a computer program or phone app, there are things that must be in there. Make a note of the date, the venue, the exact time period you fished, and the state of the tide: whether it was either side of dead low water, low water through to high water, half tide to full tide, over high water, or down the ebbing outgoing tide. Add the wind direction and speed, and if the wind veered while fishing. Was there cloud cover, or was it sunny, daylight or darkness? Was there a moon, and, if so, at what stage of the moon cycle was it? Record the sea state and surf conditions. If you were rock fishing, was there a slight, medium or heavy sea swell running? Note the clarity of the water, and was there any weed present?

Make a note of anything unusual you come across, such as jellyfish in larger than normal numbers indicating warmer sea temperatures. Also, areas on the beach where you notice more debris and weed has collected, and changes in the shape and contours of the beach that suggest a tidal currents influence.

Also record all your catches. Note the species, what rigs they were caught on, what baits, and as much other information as you can, such as on what state of the incoming or outgoing tide you caught them. This is why a diary is hard work, but the information is a huge factor in how well you will do in the future. The more you can record, the more patterns, over time, you will see. This knowledge then comes together and you learn to recognise exactly which beach, rock mark or other venue will fish best in the prevailing wind direction and sea conditions during specific times of year. It also helps to pinpoint exactly when bigger fish are present and in what weather pattern and tide size. Always remember that fish, in general, are predictable. They come and go pretty much at the same times of year, feed in the same hotspots, and favour certain conditions. Never underestimate the power of your diary. It will become your bible and an indispensable part of your tactical fishing.

Research is not, then, just something you do at the outset. I've found that research is a constant ongoing thing for me. As your fishing interests develop, the amount of research needed also increases. It becomes like a side hobby that often proves to be nearly as much fun as the actual fishing. It's a little like the sportsman finding more and more success the more he practises. The more research and fishing time you put in, and the more information you record, over time, the more you will catch, and that's a guarantee!

Chapter 3: Weather Patterns and How To Read Them

The term 'fair weather fisherman' is one to note. If you favour only fishing when the weather is warm, sunny and calm, your chances of catching will be much reduced. Food is not easily found by fish. They have to work for it. Either by chasing it down if it's a live prey fish, or by working the seabed to physically find dead or dying food. Fish that are feeding on the seabed need some water movement to help wash buried worms and shellfish out of the sand, or flush crabs out from under rocks and from inside weed bed growth. This is one reason why flat calm seas are normally difficult to fish, because the fish are not there in numbers due to a lack of washed out food.

Understanding weather patterns and how they affect and distribute the fish is an integral part of our tactical approach to angling. Some of you may be tempted to skip this chapter. I strongly suggest you don't! This is one of the most important chapters of the book. I've found in my own fishing that an understanding of the weather patterns, which allows you to decipher the weather forecasts in greater detail, gives you the ability to better predict which marks and venues will fish, and exactly when they will fish, and for what species.

THE JET STREAM

Jet streams are present in both the Northern and Southern Hemispheres and have a major influence on the world's weather. The UK's weather is directly governed by the jet stream flowing across the Northern Hemisphere; that, in turn, influences our fishing prospects, so understanding this high wind current effect can improve your catches.

The jet stream is a body of air, ribbon-like, flowing west to east high up in the atmosphere. It is situated between the troposphere and the stratosphere approximately 7 miles above the surface of the earth at the poles, and some 10 miles above the surface at the equator. It flows at a speed of about 100mph, but can reach 200mph.

THE JET STREAM

Jet streams form and flow strongest in two zones where variable air temperature gradients are steepest. For example, across the boundary between polar and mid-latitude air, which creates the polar-front jet or polar jet. Also the boundary between mid-latitude air and tropical air, called the subtropical jet.

The jets usually act independently, but can sometimes join together across an area of the earth. The polar jet is the strongest as the temperature gradient across the polar and mid-latitude regions is greatest. This further increases in the Northern Hemisphere during the winter period.

Landmasses and the Coriolis effect influence the directional flow of the jet stream as it moves over the earth like a flowing river. As air moves from high to low pressure in the Northern Hemisphere, it is deflected to the right by the Coriolis force. In the Southern Hemisphere, air moving from high to low pressure is deflected to the left by the Coriolis force. Landmasses interrupt the flow of the jet stream through friction and temperature differences, with the spin of the earth also enhancing these changes.

In winter, the temperature of the stratosphere is also affected by the strength and position of the jet stream. The cooler the polar stratosphere is, the stronger the polar and tropical differential becomes with the jet stream gaining strength. Also the warmth of landmasses and oceans can have a bearing on the strength of the jet stream.

Stronger areas of the jet stream are called jet streaks. These designate areas where the speed of the jet stream has increased by up to 60mph. These areas are about 100 miles wide, some 1 to 2 miles thick, and several hundred kilometres in length. The stronger jet streaks occur where the upper air differentials are greatest. Consequently, the weakest jet streaks occur where the temperature differentials are weakest. Strong jet streaks wander less in direction than weaker ones.

When the jet stream is flowing fast, straight and strong with minimal wandering, the UK will have weather coming straight in off the open Atlantic. This will typically be wet, windy and with average temperatures. Good examples were the persistent and severe gales and storms during the winters of 2013/14, and again in 2015/16. Both of these winters saw exceptional rainfall as well.

During periods when the jet stream amplifies, polar air travels further south than normal, and subtropical air travels further north. The exact position of the amplification determines whether the UK will be in cold polar air or warmer air from the south. If this situation becomes stagnant the UK may experience either of these conditions for a period of time. This is commonly called a 'block'.

If the polar jet is well to the south of the UK it will be colder than average weather. If the jet is to the north of the UK, the weather will be warmer than average. With the polar jet situated right over the UK, the weather will be wet and windier than average. If the polar jet has a large amplification, cold air will travel further south than average and warm air will travel further north than average. And finally, the direction and angle of the jet stream as it arrives over the UK determines whether we get cold, dry, warm, or wet weather from the Atlantic or continental sources.

If you look at the position of the jet stream in relation to the UK, using the above information will help you predict what the weather patterns are likely to be.

WARM AND COLD WEATHER FRONTS

Watch the weather forecasts on TV and you'll often hear reference to 'warm' and 'cold' fronts. These are usually shown on coloured weather charts as a series of half circles in red for warm fronts, and blue forward-facing triangles to represent cold fronts.

Warm fronts are formed when advancing warm air climbs over a mass of cold air. As the warm air lifts into regions of lower pressure, it expands, cools and condenses the water vapour, forming wide, flat sheets of cloud. With a cold front, the cold air moves underneath the warm air which is pushed upwards and creates heavy rain.

A WARM FRONT

Warm fronts are associated with low-pressure systems and are the boundary line between warm air behind the warm front line and cold air in front of it as the warm front advances forwards. Warm fronts, then, bring milder air conditions, but also often induce a spell of prolonged rain too, though this is typically light drizzle, but can also be moderate accumulations of rain. This coincides with initially cloudy, grey skies, though these will clear relatively quickly to clear skies.

It is no surprise that cold fronts are basically the reverse of warm fronts, with cold air to the rear of the divide line and warm air in front of it as the cold front moves forwards. As a cold front advances it normally brings an initial period of heavy rain as the warm air is pushed upwards, but this will soon dissipate to clearer skies with sunny spells, or mixed periods of sun and showers. In the summer, a cold front can also induce thundery conditions as the cold air starts to mix with the warm air. Watch out for cold fronts in winter though, as these often trigger a spell of cold, snowy conditions, or a brief period of heavy rain. Cold fronts are also associated with low-pressure systems.

A COLD FRONT

There is a third front, an occluded front, that is a mix of both a warm and cold front. This is created when a warm and cold front collide and start to mix. However, one of the fronts will tend to be dominant. So if the warm front is stronger this will act like a warm front, but if it is a cold occluded front, then it will be more like a cold front in behaviour. These occluded fronts are also married to low-pressure systems and will bring changeable weather. An occluded front will be shown by either an alternate mixed series of semi circles in red and triangles in blue, or both those symbols in purple, which is the basic colour you achieve if you mix red and blue.

By understanding the difference between warm, cold and occluded fronts, we can predict the likely levels and rough time span of rain, and even forecast potential localised snowfall too, as well as low-pressure systems moving in. Low-pressure systems often give ideal conditions for cod and bass as the sea and surf movement increases to expose more food.

ANTICYCLONES

The weather forecasts will often refer to anticyclones, or high-pressure systems, and these are important for anglers to understand as they forecast light winds and calm seas, but can also predict fog and frost.

Anticyclones only have one type of air mass, but this covers a large geographical area and does not have either a warm or cold front. The area an anticyclone can cover is huge and can typically be in excess of 2000 miles. Once an anticyclone becomes established it becomes dominant and can settle in over a large area and control the weather pattern for several days or more. The wind pattern will be light to calm and move clockwise around the centre of the anticyclone. This is shown on the weather charts by widely spaced isobars circling the centre of the anticyclone with the barometric pressure readings high.

TYPICAL SUMMER ANTICYCLONE

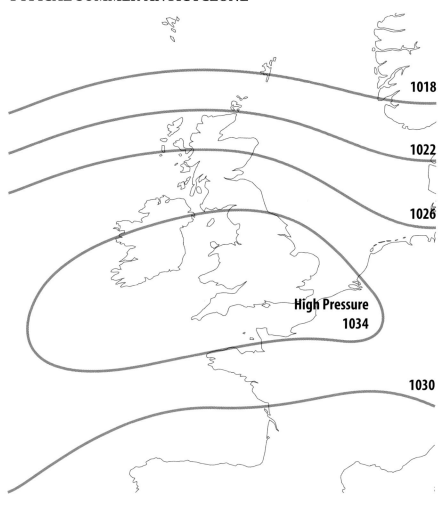

Anticyclones are basically high-pressure systems within which the air travels downwards towards the earth's surface. As the air descends, the molecules become compressed and tightened, the pressure then increases and the air warms. When the air is warming, moisture in the atmosphere is evaporated, which means no clouds can form, producing clear sunny skies and settled weather.

In the UK an anticyclone in mid-summer will mean very warm weather during the day with temperatures likely to be in the mid to high 20s (degrees Celsius). However, at night, because there are no clouds to act as a shield, heat will quickly be lost. Because the ground then cools, this creates the condensation of water vapour in the descending warm air, causing heavy dew on the ground and mist. Both of these will clear quickly come morning as the warmth from the sun's rays reheats the ground. After a few days of anticyclonic weather, a layer of hot air builds up at ground level. This layer of hot air will eventually create thunderstorms that will end the dominance of the anticyclone and change the weather pattern away from the anticyclone's influence. The period just prior to thunderstorms can be good for surf tope, if the tides are rising towards high springs with low water in the late afternoon or evening.

During the winter, though, the longer hours of darkness coupled with clear cloudless skies creates rapid cooling of the ground. With this there is a major risk of dew, frost and also thick fog patches which can be persistent and be slow to clear during the day. In very calm windless conditions the fog and frost can linger for several days or more. Air quality is also affected as with little air movement any air pollution is held at low levels producing smog like conditions. This weather pattern can produce difficult shore fishing with bites few and far between.

Something else to watch out for is an anticyclone becoming anchored over northern Europe during the winter. If this occurs, then most of the UK will be affected by very cold easterly winds that blow in from Siberia. These easterly winds tend to affect the fishing with bites at a premium if the bitterly cold conditions persist, especially on the west lee coasts where the sea conditions will be flat and the water clarity rapidly turning gin-clear. This especially applies to areas where the beaches are shallow where light penetration through the clear water will push fish well offshore and make even night time fishing difficult, again with bites at a premium.

UNDERSTANDING ISOBARS

Isobars are very important to sea anglers. No idea what an isobar is? They are the roughly circular, concentric, white bands you see on the TV and internet weather charts identifying low- and high-pressure systems approaching across the Atlantic, or weather systems passing over the UK. These, at a glance, give you a pretty good idea whether the winds will be strong or light, and from what direction the winds will blow from. Being able to read what the isobars are doing gives you an early insight in to where might fish best several days before you even intend to go fishing.

In simple terms an isobar is a symbolic line joining areas of equal atmospheric pressure. Look closely at the lines and you will see a number close to them that increases or decreases by four with each isobar. The number measures the atmospheric pressure in millibars. A millibar is 0.02953 inches of mercury. If you listen to the Shipping Forecast carefully you will hear the presenter say something like, "1002 millibars, and falling".

As an example, an anti-cyclone high-pressure system bringing settled weather and calm conditions could see a reading of as much as 1050 millibars, whereas a low reading of 960 millibars would be an exceptionally low-pressure system with severe gale force winds. Average readings in the UK fall typically somewhere between 980 millibars and 1020 millibars, with the average sea-level pressure reading being 1013 millibars. A reading taken at the centre of a deep depression could drop as low as 950 millibars, though 930 millibars has been recorded in the past in the UK. The isobars readings are always adjusted to sea level, with any differences due to altitude being ignored.

If you study an area of high pressure, the millibar numbers will be highest in the centre of the innermost circle formed by the isobar lines, with the numbers on the lines forming the outside edge of the isobar circle getting gradually lower. As a low-pressure system advances towards the UK, the innermost circle of the isobars will have the lower reading, with the isobars on the outside showing the higher reading. When the presenter on the Shipping Forecast says, "998 millibars and falling", he is telling us that the pressure is falling, indicating the likelihood of deteriorating weather and increasing winds. If he says, "998 millibars and rising", this is obviously a rising pressure system more likely to bring improving weather and lighter winds.

What is crucial to anglers is how the isobars form together. When isobars are shown well spread apart, then wind strengths will be light. The tighter together the isobars are on the chart, then the higher the wind strength will be, and heavy rain is likely too. The isobars will be tightest around the centre of the depression, which identifies which specific area in the country, or your region, will see the strongest winds. You can see this when watching the TV weather charts, or check out the pressure charts on the internet. This tells us instantly if the marks we want to fish fall in the high or low wind sector, and whether they will be fishable;

also, which beaches will have the biggest surf, and those that sit in the sheltered lee side of the wind. If isobars are formed in longer straight lines over a wider geographical area, then expect stronger winds.

LOW PRESSURE SYSTEM ISOBARS OVER THE UK

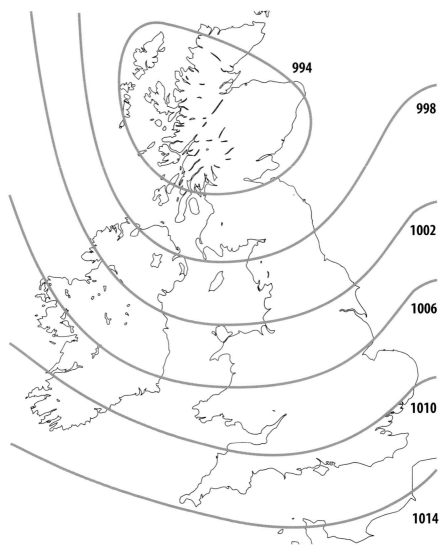

Shore anglers who learn about isobars are also able to identify little windows of calmer weather as the depression passes through when the isobars are that little bit wider, or when the calmer eye of the depression is briefly overhead, indicating brief periods when the sea remains wild and rough, but the wind drops. These short periods often produce big catches of bass and cod.

An interesting thing to know is that in the Northern Hemisphere, including the UK, winds blow anti-clockwise around an approaching low pressure system, but clockwise around an advancing high pressure system. The wind also flows in an almost parallel line with the shown isobars, allowing us to forecast the wind direction as the system passes over the UK.

As you can see, understanding isobars, those simple little white lines on the weather charts, can dramatically improve our ability as anglers to predict when and where to fish for the best results.

HOW BAROMETRIC PRESSURE CHANGES AFFECT FISH

One of the best tools an angler can buy is a barometer. It does not need to be anything fancy or expensive, just a serviceable clock-type barometer. These need to be positioned, though, on an internal but outside-facing wall to get accurate readings. Some of the new electronic 'weather stations' available are also good, giving a wide variety of information.

Arguably, the barometer is by far the simplest and best though. It is used to indicate rising and falling barometric pressure, which has a major effect on when fish will feed, but also when they choose not to feed.

If you get in to the habit of checking the barometer every day, you will see the indicator needle move upwards clockwise to indicate rising pressure, and fall anti-clockwise to show falling pressure. If you gently tap the face of the barometer, the needle will naturally adjust, and give you an instant indication of whether pressure is rising or falling. There are also word indicators on the inner face that tells you, by pressure readings, what sort of weather to expect. The word *Change* is commonly used as the in-between marker, with rising pressure given first as *Fair*, then *Very Dry*. As pressure falls and the needle drops left of *Change*, it will read *Rain* then *Stormy*.

A fish feels changes in the barometric pressure through its swim bladder. Fish with small swim bladders are affected less by pressure change than fish with bigger swim bladders, the body density of smaller fish being closer to that of the surrounding water.

Fish with larger swim bladders quickly feel dropping air pressure. As the pressure drops, the pressure on their swim bladders lessens, which

causes the bladder to expand. This causes discomfort to these fish. They respond to this discomfort by dropping deeper in the water column to stabilize that pressure, or by absorbing extra gas into their swim bladders. However, many food items they feed on will have swim bladders too, and this in turn will affect where and when the bigger predators feed as their target baitfish also adjust depth by going deeper.

This increased stress means they have little interest in feeding. Their prime thought is to find a depth at which they feel comfortable and can adjust their swim bladder accordingly. Think rock ledge pollack here. When you go on a rock one day and hit fish after fish, then go the next day and they prove reluctant to feed, this is one of the most probable causes, that a change in barometric pressure has forced the fish deeper and tighter to the seabed, and made them less likely to feed. This is also why some days the pollack take lures within the first 15 feet of the seabed, but not higher, and on other days they work the mid water column 40 feet or more up off the seabed.

Shore lure anglers will also notice a change when bass fishing and using surface poppers. One day, the bass hit the surface poppers; the next day, you need to fish deeper with a deep diving plug to take a fish. Dropping pressure has probably forced the bass, and baitfish, deeper. This also explains why during periods of bad weather and storms, even in deeper water, ledger fishing can be poor at best. The low pressure subdues the fish's feeding instinct.

During rising pressure, and periods when high pressure is stable, the fish will feed throughout the water column, and quite actively most of the time.

A typical scenario is during settled pressure that does not change rapidly; the fishing remains consistent, often good. Then you see the barometer needle backing anti-clockwise, indicating a cold front is heading our way. Ahead of this front is low pressure. The fish sense the forthcoming change in pressure and will feed heavily right up until the point the pressure actually starts to drop quickly, then change their feeding habits going deeper and slowly eating less and less to a point when few if any fish feed at all.

As the front passes through and high pressure reasserts itself, it can take at least three or four tides before the fish start to feed aggressively again. This is the time it takes for the fish to readjust their swim bladders. However, after those few tides have passed, the fish can go on a feeding binge and some great catches can be enjoyed. This is often the third day after the pressure starts to rebuild.

So far, man's understanding of the science behind fish's reactions to changing weather patterns and pressure systems remains limited. There is currently major work in hand in the USA looking at this, but it will likely be years yet before real conclusions are made. Basic observation passed down by previous generations has alerted us to the facts we do already know today and prove accurate within the scope of normal angling.

As anglers, work and family commitments mean we often have to go fishing as and when we can, immaterial of what the weather is doing. Those of you with more freedom to act spontaneously: if you can use the barometer to predict what fish might do as pressure changes then you will see an upturn in catches. Yes, there are many factors that dictate whether we catch, such as food availability, wind direction, tide size, and much more, but do not ignore the pressure readings, as these play a vital role too.

WELL-KNOWN WEATHER SAYINGS

There are many sayings related to weather observations that have been passed down by our ancestors. Some are even quoted in biblical writings. People of previous ages, with no technology, had only their eyes and experience to judge what the weather was about to do, and critical decisions regards hunting, fishing, crop planting and harvesting relied heavily on these sayings.

Even in this day of so-called highly technical weather forecasting, the sayings of old can help anglers decipher what is about to happen and help put us on to the right marks at the right time.

The most famous saying of all is 'Red sky at night: shepherd's delight. Red sky in the morning: shepherd takes warning'. Red sky at sunset forecasts a period of dry, settled weather with a likelihood of high pressure bringing calm, settled sea conditions. You need to look for red sky around the sun, not red reflecting off the clouds. As the sun rises at a low angle in the east, it can reflect off cloud in the west predicting a weather front moving in and bringing deteriorating weather and rain, hence the shepherd takes warning.

An important one for anglers to learn is, 'Seagull, seagull sat on the sand, it's never fine weather when you're on the land'. Seagulls know when poor weather is coming in from the Atlantic and will sit on the sand facing in to the exact direction the bad weather and strong winds will come from. This occurs about 24 hours before it hits. Very useful to know and an indicator to seek sheltered marks if you intend to fish the next day.

Very accurate, though little used nowadays is, 'In the morning, mountains; come afternoon, fountains'. This is an observation of cumulus clouds building in the morning as ground level heat increases and the air heats up. If the atmospheric conditions are right, the clouds increase quickly in size and form a mushroom shape. Come the afternoon, these clouds will extend right up to the upper atmosphere and will bring rain and probably thunder. Thundery conditions are rarely good for general fishing.

Sometimes quoted by TV weather forecasters is another well-known verse: 'When the wind is in the east, 'tis neither good for man nor beast'. This is allied to our worst weather generally coming from the east. Heavy snow and ice is highly likely in the UK when a bitterly cold and strengthening east wind blows straight in from Russia and Siberia. The east coast usually gets the worst of it too. In summer, though, east winds bring poor air quality with hazy skies. East winds, even for commercial fisherman, tend to bring a reduction in catches the longer they blow. The maritime fishing version goes, 'When the wind is in the east, the fish bite the least", and it's generally correct.

Also very accurate is the verse, 'If a circle forms 'round the moon, 'twill rain or snow very soon'. The frontal edge or top structure of an incoming weather front will often be seen on the far horizon, or high in the sky, hours before the weather front actually hits. The cloud layer is thin, fuzzy, or hazy, formed from ice crystals called cirrostratus. When viewed at night, these ice crystals create what is called a lunar corona, or circle of colour, around the moon. This sign tells you rain is imminent, and, in winter, possibly snow.

Though maybe not as reliable as the others quoted above, 'Rain before seven, fine by eleven' is often used. This is based on the fact that low-pressure weather systems move across the UK fairly quickly due to the predominantly westerly airflow coming in off the Atlantic. This relies on a weather front moving through during the morning, bringing better weather behind it. Sometimes, though, it can rain all night and most of the day, rendering this saying less reliable, but it's more often right than not.

Passed down by untold generations, never ignore these sayings, for, as we've seen, they are based on centuries of observation by people who relied on just their eyesight and day-to-day experience to survive. Modern weather forecasts will always have the edge, but knowing these sayings can help predict what is about to come, especially when you're actually fishing, or about to go fishing.

HOW WIND AFFECTS THE MOVEMENT OF FISH

Many factors dictate the movement of inshore feeding or travelling fish. The availability of food and the direction of the tide being two obvious ones, but equally important is the direction and strength of the wind and how this effects the state of the sea.

A common phrase in fishing is to 'look for an onshore wind'. Actually, a wind blowing straight on to shore creates surf across the full length of the beach and this will displace food relatively equally within the inner surf tables, and along the whole tidal edge. In these conditions the fish are also naturally well spread out along the full length of the beach. This means you will be targeting fish that are constantly travelling to actively search out their food. In effect you are fishing for passers-by, not fish grouped up and feeding in a relatively small area. This tells us that, generally, a direct onshore wind is a good fishing wind, but it does not necessarily create the conditions to give the best catches.

Talk to long-in-the-tooth bass anglers and they will tell you that they prefer a crosswind. To explain this, we'll use a generally west-facing surf beach as an example.

With the beach facing due west, a southwest wind will angle across the beach. Typically, many beaches have rocky cliffs or headlands at each corner. In this situation, with the southwest wind, the southern corner of the beach will be calmest. Generally speaking, the chances of catching fish in this southern section are more limited as food is less likely to have been exposed due to the lack of surf action. Fish look for areas of surf and sea swell that will displace food, and with this crosswind the rougher seas will be from the middle of the beach heading north in to the north corner of the beach. The surf here will be greater and increase proportionately as you near the northern corner, and this greater movement of water will expose much more food from the sand. Expect the greatest concentration of fish to be right in the north corner where the majority of the displaced food will collect.

If the wind is coming from the northwest corner, then the opposite will apply, with the north corner calm, and the southern corner carrying surf and swell, and holding the majority of any feeding fish. This crosswind situation applies just the same for beaches that face south, east, or in any other direction, with the corners facing into the wind being the fish hotspots.

CROSSWIND SITUATION

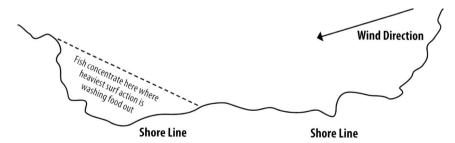

Fish concentrate here where heaviest surf action is washing food out

Wind Direction

Shore Line   Shore Line

This principle of identifying and fishing moving water is also relevant when fishing man-made structures, such as harbour walls, breakwaters and solid jetties. Always fish the wind side for the most consistent sport, and this especially applies to predators such as pollack and bass.

Structures, such as breakwaters and small groynes on beaches, are also prone to wind direction. If you watch a crosswind blow against a wooden groyne, it creates wave and swell on the wind side, but it remains calm on the downwind side. All manner of fish, bass, flounder, dabs, sole, plaice *etc* will work or sit on the windward side and pick off any food that gets pushed in or washed off the groyne by wave and water action. Often, with a persistent wind, sand gets washed away from the base of the groyne, creating a deeper gutter, which again will trap and hold food washed in.

It also applies when fishing estuaries, for although the fish will use the main channel and side creeks for initial travelling, the majority will hunt and feed on the side the wind hits. Bass are particularly active on estuary edges with wave action present as crabs and small fish, such as shannies and butterfish, get washed out from under weed and stones. This also tells us that short casts, sometimes literally just a rod length out, will be the best place to position baits.

Winds that blow off the land and flatten the sea obviously kill any obvious surf action, bar natural sea swell. However, if you can get some height, say off the top of a sand dune, or better still from rocks or roads looking down on to the beach, then you may see some small areas of short choppy wave action. You may not see this from beach level as the waves are travelling and rolling over in a direction away from you, but with height it will be obvious. This chop on the water is caused by shallower ground, typically a bank formed either side of a deeper channel running parallel with the beach that funnels the tide. The offshore wind pushes water back against the forward facing edge of the bank and forms the chop. This is a good place to look for bass, flounder, dabs and even rays when the wind is offshore. This will concentrate the fish within this small area. Fish a short way away from this and you may well be putting baits in to a dead spot with no bites forthcoming.

When you have no option, or deliberately want to fish directly in to an offshore wind, this is when distance casting can really pay off. The water immediately inshore is usually protected and in the lee of the land, so is flat. A short way out the lee is lost and the wind hits the water's surface. Again from a height, you will see a definite demarcation line where this water loses the calm and roughens up. This is where you need to drop your baits. Fish work along this line picking off food that is displaced by the more agitated water.

Applying just a little thought, then, as to how the wind is hitting the beach on the day, adjusting your position to take advantage of where the best surf and swell is breaking will dramatically increase your chances of catching fish.

You will find that, as your tactical thought progresses, so too will your powers of observation. This comes with time and experience, but over time you will come to notice little differences in surface water shape that give a clue to a change of seabed or a tidal current that will further sway those odds more in your favour.

WEED AND HOW TO AVOID IT

Weed is the curse of all shore anglers. It can make your fishing time frustrating, laborious when constantly picking weed off the line, and it can often prove impossible to fish as the amount of weed on the line pulls the terminal tackle free and washes it downtide. However, a little understanding of how weed moves with the tide and the wind can minimise the problem and help see you successfully fish when others go home frustrated.

BEACHES

Imagine a west coast beach facing westerly. It has rocky cliffs that jut out at the southern end and a low rocky headland at the northern end. The tide flow on the flood is left to right in direction.

After a period of rough seas when weed has been ripped from reefs and rough ground offshore, a southwesterly wind and flooding tide will push the weed inshore, but it will be most prevalent from the middle of this beach travelling northward and in to the northern corner. In these conditions the very southern end of the beach, where the rocky cliffs are, will carry minimal weed and is likely to be more easily and effectively fished.

WEED AND HOW TO AVOID IT

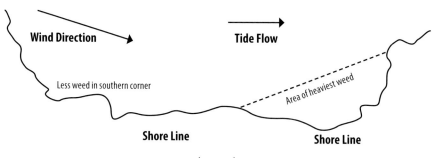

In a northwest wind, exactly the opposite will occur as the weed tends to float in the upper surface layers and will be blown and washed in to the southern corner, leaving the northern corner relatively weed-free.

If the wind is blowing straight in to the beach, then on the flood tide the northern corner will still collect the majority of the weed which will be tide–borne, leaving the southern corner more fishable. On the ebb tide, though, the weed in the northern corner is left high and dry on the beach or shingle making it the better option to fish. The ebb tide will carry the waterborne weed in a southerly direction with some of it ending up in the southern corner.

To give an example for a beach on the south coast, a flooding tide from the south quarter and a wind from the southwest would see a beach facing south weeded out in the east corner, but probably fishable in the west corner. Switch the wind to the east and weed would collect in the west corner and be relatively weed free on the east side. The angles of wind and tide generally apply to any beach facing any direction.

An east-facing beach on a flood tide sees the weed collect in the north corner with a south to southeast wind blowing, but the south corner collects the weed when the wind is in the northeast and the tide is ebbing. An east wind blowing directly on to the beach will see the tide flow dictate where the weed collects, typically in the corner the tide is flowing in to.

One last thing to look for are small washup areas on the shingle or sand at high water. These are areas where flotsam and jetsam collect, as well as weed. These show where small tidal currents, particular to that beach, wash ashore, bringing with them greater accumulations of weed. Noting where these are and avoiding them can also see you less frustrated with weed on the line than other anglers nearby.

ESTUARIES

The movement of weed inside estuaries is pretty much constant and it is much harder to locate areas that will allow some fishing.

Firstly, avoid fishing the deeper main channels as these are the weed motorways. Ignore any deeper scoured-out areas as weed falls in to these by gravity and it can be several feet deep at times with heavy weed. Also try to fish either side of low or high water when the tide flow is minimised and the weed is less mobile and semi-settled on the seabed.

Another good tip is to fish on the downtide side of any back eddies that form alongside the main channel current. These are often created by an uplifting sandbank or finger of rock that juts out in to the tide. The weed gets drawn in to the back eddy, but the water immediately below can almost be weed free as the vortex of the eddy traps and holds the weed.

Flat, shallow areas can be weed infested, but if you can find access to the edge of a deeper channel with a short cast that keeps your line right on the outer edge of the bank but in deeper water, then you minimise weed problems but maintain a high chance of fish finding the bait. The more vertical your line, the less likelihood there is for weed to collect on it.

In the seaward mouths of smaller estuaries, such as those found in the West Country and in West Wales, the tidal current can often run strongest down one side of the estuary mouth on the flood tide, but then strongest on the opposite side on the ebb tide. Typically, the strongest flow will be on the side of the estuary facing towards the oncoming tide by direction. On the ebb, the tide takes the shortest route and will hug the side the tide will cross over as it ebbs towards the southern quarter.

The movement of weed in relation to the wind and tide is thankfully fairly predictable, and knowing this basic information can save hours of wasted fishing time, with yet again fish far more likely to be caught at a time when the majority of anglers will be totally defeated simply because they chose the wrong place to fish.

This is why I set so much store on understanding the weather. It predicts where the fish are likely to be, whether we can actually fish, and when may be the best time to fish. It also minimizes lost time fishing in to heavy or weed infested seas.

SEA TEMPERATURE

This is difficult area to understand and decipher as sea temperatures can fluctuate year to year according to weather patterns, and sometimes can be quite localised too, especially where cold estuary water floods directly in to the sea.

Looking at sea temperatures in general, and starting early in the year, it is around late February that overall sea temperatures reach their lowest point. Depending on locality, the lowest normal sea temperatures fall between 6 and 10 degrees Celsius around this time. The coldest reading is in the North Sea, with the far south and west coasts of the UK and Ireland having a higher reading due to the influence of the warming Gulf Stream. That said, sea temperatures in the south are always warmer than those in the north, even off the west coast of the UK.

Due to the increasing hours of daylight, and more so, hopefully, increasing hours of sunshine, the water is slowly warmed as each week and month passes as we head through spring and in to summer. Even cloudy days put some heat in to the water, as the cloud ceiling stops heat escaping.

Sea temperatures normally peak around late September at between 14 and 20 degrees Celsius depending on your geographical location, the latter in exceptionally good weather years and in the extreme south. Thereafter they gradually fall towards their lowest point again in February.

Obviously sea temperatures have a bearing on fish, but it's not simply a direct temperature link. It's no coincidence that the majority of fish are out spawning in deeper water when the sea temperatures hit rock bottom for the year, in February. Offshore, the greater depth of water maintains a more consistent temperature without erratic fluctuation that is the norm inshore. And it's equally no coincidence that they start to return inshore around late March and April when the sea temperature is rapidly rising due to the increased daylight hours. The warming water at this time, usually when its approaching 10 to 11 degrees Celsius, seems to trigger the first really big explosions of peeling crab, plus the sandeel move back inshore and in to the outer estuary channels, and the mackerel start shoaling up inshore. With a food supply readily available, the fish naturally come back to capitalise on that and fatten back up after the rigours of spawning.

As the sea temperatures peak in September, so the autumn species, such as the whiting and the cod, are triggered to move back inshore. This is also governed by the decreasing daylight hours, with the extended hours of darkness more favourable for these fish to hunt inshore. Plus, the autumnal gales occur around this period, again encouraging these fish to move in and take food churned out by the stormy seas. There is an overlap of summer and winter species through until roughly mid November when the summer fish have mostly moved out for deeper water.

Individual fish can be affected by heat and cold. For example, stingray are best fished for in May and June. Ideally you need to choose a tide time when low water falls in the early afternoon, and pick a hot, sunny day, with little wind. During the morning and early afternoon, the sun heats the sand and mud exposed by low water. As the new tide floods in, the hot sand heats up the shallow water, making the heat-loving stingray move in to lap up the heat within easy casting range. Pick an overcast day with a strong, chilly, offshore wind, and the stingray stay way out in deeper water where the temperature is more consistent. Bass, mullet, black bream, gilthead bream, flounder, and plaice are other obvious fish that actively seek out shallow, warmer water as and when it's available.

This works in reverse in very cold weather. When there is a period of prolonged heavy frost, the shallow sand cools right down. As the new flood tide progresses, this sees the shallow water temperature cool too. In these conditions, fish often choose to stay out in deeper water, somewhere in proximity to the mean low water tide line, where the cooling of the sand is not a factor as it's insulated by the depth of constant water. Cod are typically prone to opting for staying in deeper water if the inshore sandy shallows are heavily frosted, or, worse still, in extreme cases, the inner surf tables are carrying ice and trying to freeze. Cod anglers have often noted that cod will suddenly switch on and feed when it starts to snow after a period of bitterly cold, dry weather. This is because the temperature rises as it snows and the fish feel the change in the weather. Fish are sensitive creatures and need to acclimatize, they cannot instantly adapt.

Summertime triggerfish always tend to be found close to rock outcrops or under wooden jetties. Yes, they seek out natural protective cover where food will be located too; but the rocks and the stone and timber jetties naturally heat up with the heat of the sun, and this heat is transferred, in part, to the immediate surrounding seawater. The triggerfish take up station here because the water is a fraction warmer. Bass also like shallow stony ground to hunt over, especially in the spring. Again, this is because the heat of the sun is held in the stone; then, as the tide floods, this warms the water a little more, making it more comfortable for the bass. These 'hot spots' will also see more food available in the form of crabs and small fish.

Early and late in the year, I try to avoid fishing too near freshwater inflows that spill on to a beach. This cools the seawater in the immediate vicinity and can push fish away. The exception would be in very hot summer conditions during big tides when the sun really warms up a large expanse of sand between low and high tide lines, and in turn the new flooding tide as it floods the sand. This influx of cooler, oxygenated freshwater can see bass and flounder in particular linger here and use the slight mixing and cooling of the surrounding seawater to help them acclimatize before moving on.

You may not read this information in scientific books based on commercially targeted species, but anglers have independently learnt these things by time and observation. We may be unique in that we see and (to a greater or lesser extent!) understand these things!

Chapter 4: The Tides

Tides are vitally important to shore anglers. They govern the movement and whereabouts of fish, dictate when and how we collect bait, and in many areas govern the actual marks we are able to access and fish. The creation of tides sounds complicated, but a basic understanding of how the tides work is relatively easy.

ALIGNMENT OF SUN, MOON & EARTH CREATING SPRING TIDES

Not to scale

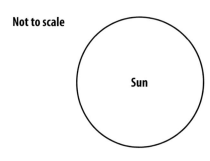

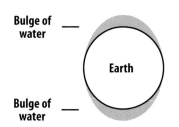

Bulge of water —

Bulge of water —

The UK has what are called semi-diurnal tides; that is, two high tides and two low tides per day.

Tides are caused by the effects of gravity within the earth, moon and sun configuration and the planet's movements. A good way to understand this is to imagine that the earth is totally covered in water.

There are two outward bulges of water, one pulled towards the moon on one side of the earth, and another on the opposite side of the earth created by the earth's centrifugal rotation. The rise and fall in sea levels are caused by the earth rotating on its axis underneath these bulges of water. There are two tides every day because the earth passes under the two bulges as it rotates within its 24-hour cycle. These are called lunar tides.

Two additional bulges of water are also caused by the sun, and are called solar tides. These work with the lunar tide during the new and full moon period as the earth, moon and sun are generally in line and both bulges of water then coincide in the same place on the earth's surface creating the larger spring tides.

When the earth, sun and moon are at a right angle to each other and the direct pull is much reduced, the high water caused by the lunar tide coincides with the low water of the solar tide and gives us the smaller neap tides.

ALIGNMENT OF SUN, MOON AND EARTH DURING NEAP TIDES

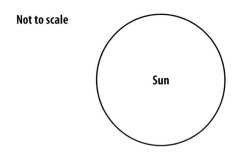

Incidentally, the phrase 'spring' tide has nothing to do with the season of the year, and the word 'neap' tides is thought to originate from the Middle English word 'neep' meaning small.

You might wonder why the time of high water is not the same all around the UK. The difference in tide times is due to the land mass getting in the way of the moving tidal current. As the earth rotates, water moves over the earth's surface to create the high tides, but there is a time delay due to the shape of the coastline and the differences in overall sea depth. With all areas of coastline having different physical terrain and massively varied depths, it is this that gives each area its own specific tidal pattern.

The highest tides of the year fall a day or two after the full and new moon nearest to the spring equinox, usually around March 20th/21st, and the autumn equinox on the 22nd/23rd of September. The equinox is when the tilt of the earth's axis is angled neither away from, nor towards the sun, the centre of the sun being in the same plane as the earth's equator.

Tides occur roughly every 12 hours and 25 minutes in the UK. It is not exactly 12 hours, or half the time of an earth day as you might expect. This is due to the moon also orbiting around the earth and exerting its effect on the bulge of water requiring the earth to rotate for an extra 25 minutes to compensate to be directly under the high water bulge.

That is all there is to the creation of tides. Once you understand the earth's rotation and the bulges of water, the rest is easy!

TIDES FOR FISHING

Tides are classified, officially, as neap tides and spring tides. The neap tides are the tides that have the smallest rise between the mean low and high water marks. These fall just after the first and third quarter moon when the moon and sun are at right angles to each other, the solar tide helping to partially negate the lunar tide.

On the spring tides, which have the greater movement between the mean low and high water marks and fall during the full and new moon periods, the sun, moon and earth are in a degree of alignment, maximising the gravitational pull to create higher high tides and lower low tides.

During the duration of a flooding tide, a quarter of the tidal rise occurs in the first two hours, half in the next two hours when the tidal flow is at its strongest, and the final quarter in the last two hours. It is the same on the outgoing ebb tide. The strongest flow of tide occurs roughly at the mid tide period.

During neap tides, the flow of water moving in to beaches, or up estuaries, is lessened. In areas of fast tides where a tide flow is concentrated, such as an estuary channel or deep water beach with a lateral tidal current, the smaller neap tides with their reduced flow may be the only tides you can successfully fish. On the spring tides the speed of the tidal current is too fast and water pressure on the line can be so heavy that even heavy grip lead weights will not stay anchored to the seabed for more than a few minutes to allow effective fishing. On the big tides, passing weed can also be a problem.

In these circumstances, neap tides prove the best. Fish are not stupid and will only expend energy if there is a good chance of finding food. They will tolerate the lessened flow of the neap tide, but may not even try to feed in the vicinity of fast-moving water as they expend too much energy in the process, negating any real calorie gain. If you're faced with an area where fast tidal currents are the norm, then stick to the neap tides and you won't go far wrong.

The neap tides, especially on shallower clean sand surf beaches, lack the speed of tidal current to really churn food out from the sand. The likelihood of fish such as bass, cod and rays feeding is much reduced at these times. However, fish such as flounder will still work the surf as they have the flat body profile to allow them to work through the shallow water surf tables, just a few inches deep, where some food will be dislodged by wave action.

Spring tides, with more water movement and some lateral tide flow to scour the sand out and expose food from the sand, fish better for hunting fish like bass, cod and rays, as they use the greater movement of water up and down the beach to travel and cover more ground.

If you initially choose to fish well-known marks, then research information will suggest the best times to fish. However, when you start to fish locations that have little or no information written about them, you need a strategy that will compile information based on your own efforts. Start by fishing low water to high water. Then switch and fish high water to low water, on both rising and falling neap and spring tides, and in all weather conditions and wind directions. This is the only way to become familiar with what is right and wrong on the specific marks you choose to fish. The odds are, though, that the best period will be the whole, or part, of the flooding tide.

Another point to bear in mind is that, more often than not, the best fishing is on the tides that are rising in height towards the bigger tides. This increase in tide height, plus the added water movement, brings the fish inshore and with the expectancy to feed. Once the tide cycle peaks and the biggest tide passes, as each tide height lessens in the down period falling towards the smallest neap tide, the fishing tends to get less productive. This is, admittedly, a generalisation, for, as stated, some marks buck the trend and may fish better on smaller tides, but generally speaking the rising tide cycle fishes better than the falling tide cycle.

WEATHER EFFECTS ON TIDES

Wind direction and strength have a huge influence over the predicted low and high tide times given in a tide table, and can see tides push in faster than anticipated. This is very important, not just for the fishing and when you expect the best fishing to occur, but more importantly from a safety viewpoint when fishing exposed marks.

If the wind is blowing off the land, this will see the tide turn a little later than predicted as the wind is holding the tide back briefly by pushing against it.

If the wind is strong off the land, the tide also goes further out than is predicted on your tide table. This is useful knowledge for anglers as this further-than-predicted receding tide exposes more of the low water bait beds, and for a longer time than normal, allowing us extended bait-collecting time. On the bigger spring tides it also exposes black lug, white rag and razorfish beds that are infrequently exposed and rarely ever dug.

This is also a good time to check out ground feature beyond the average low water line that is only exposed on the biggest spring tides when the wind is blowing strongly offshore during high pressure systems.

A strong offshore wind over high tide sees the tide held back by the wind, so the predicted high tide height will be slightly less than predicted and the high tide time fall slightly earlier.

When a strong onshore wind blows, the low water time may be slightly sooner than predicted and not go out as far as anticipated. The wind is holding the water in and not letting it ebb as far out as predicted. However, at high tide, the actual tidal height will be higher than predicted and the precise moment of high tide will be a little later than the tide table suggests, with the wind both blowing the tide in further, but also holding it there longer before the ebb tide kicks in.

Anglers who fish remote sand bars and estuary mouths also need to be aware of this earlier-than-predicted turn of the tide when strong onshore winds are blowing. Not only will the tide turn earlier than anticipated, but it will also flood in at a faster pace. If you need to walk a long way back, being aware of these factors means you react in time and make a safe exit off the sands before gullies and gutters between you and safety fill earlier than expected with water.

The tides also govern how the wind behaves. If you take notice, you will see that a predicted wind speed change more often than not occurs at low or high water slack just before a new flood or ebb tide gets underway. This is often a strengthening wind coming with the flood tide, and a swinging and dropping wind with the ebb tide.

Slack water periods can also trigger a change in the direction of the wind with a flood tide seeing the wind back anti-clockwise and increase in speed. On the ebbing tide, a wind can turn clockwise and ease away, which is typical after a gale has gone through. These changes can be noted more locally than nationally.

It's also worth bearing in mind that a change in the direction of the wind at low water or high water can also see rain and worsening weather arrive, or better weather move in after a spell of rain or showers.

When the wind direction blows opposite to the tide flow, then the state of the sea will be rougher with higher wave activity. If the wind and tide are heading in the same direction, the sea state will be lessened and the surface flatter.

As you can see, wind and tide work together, sometimes to our benefit, sometimes working against us. By understanding a little of how they combine, we can avoid some of the pitfalls they put before us, but also make the most of the many opportunities they bring.

FISHING BY MOON PHASE

The majority of anglers use the actual tide size and time of tide as their main guide as to when to go fishing. Unwittingly they are also using the moon phase too, for as we've seen the tides are greatly influenced by the moon and its gravitational pull on the world's oceans, and to a lesser degree also by the alignment of the sun in relation to the moon. This is why I've included information on fishing by moon phase in this chapter dealing with tides.

More experienced anglers, and especially those overseas targeting big game fish such as marlin and swordfish, set great store by the actual phase of the moon and how this effects both the movement and the feeding impulse of fish. We've been slow in the UK and Europe to adapt this to our own fishing.

Research has found that certain phases of the moon coincide with periods of high feeding intensity by many fish. A good UK example is how conger eels all seem to feed over a short two- or three-day period, then go off feeding and can be near impossible to catch. This can be tied in to both tide and moon phase.

Good tide tables don't just show the times of the tide; if you look, they also show the moon phase, the time the moon rises, and when the moon sets. Understanding a little about the moon phases helps you use these to better predict when the best time to go fishing is, and when the fish are most likely to feed.

PHASES OF THE MOON

Shading indicates portion of the moon not seen

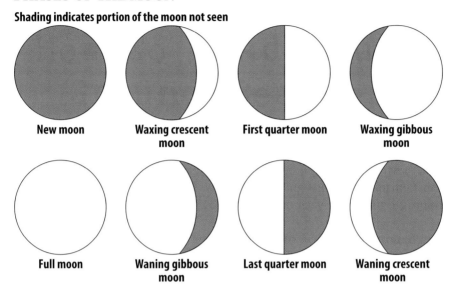

| New moon | Waxing crescent moon | First quarter moon | Waxing gibbous moon |

| Full moon | Waning gibbous moon | Last quarter moon | Waning crescent moon |

FIRST QUARTER MOON PHASE

The first quarter moon coincides with dropping neap tides. When viewed in the Northern Hemisphere and from the UK, the moon is seen with only the right-hand side visible. This is the side the sun is shining on. This quarter moon rises around midday, and sets around midnight depending on the latitude it is viewed from.

Fish will feed with the moon rising or falling, but there is strong evidence to show that the best feeding period will be when the moon is positioned midway between moon set and moon rise.

NEW MOON

A new moon is not visible as it is too close to the sun. During the new moon, if you check the tide table, you see that the moon rises around dawn, and will set near dusk.

The new moon period coincides with some of the highest tides of the monthly tidal cycle. It gives good all-round fishing with a majority of species keen to feed. Also, because there is no moonlight shining on the water on clear nights, the lack of light entering the shallows encourages smaller fish tight inshore to feed. It is no surprise, then, to find that this period often coincides with reports of big predatory fish – such as tope, huss and rays – being close in shore too.

FULL MOON

A full moon is, in a clear sky, fully visible and associated with bigger tides. It rises around dusk, and will set around dawn. It is considered a poor time to fish when the moon is up, with fish seemingly reluctant to feed. This is partly to do with moonlight shining on the water during clear skies and clear seas, but is also thought to be due to gravitational influences that fish pick up via their lateral line. The full moon is associated again with bigger tides when the influence of the moon and sun are combining.

This changes just after the moon sets and before the moon rises, and a feeding binge can trigger. How often have your heard anglers say the best fishing is towards dusk and dawn? This is one main reason why!

LAST QUARTER MOON

The last quarter moon indicates that tide heights will be falling from spring tides to smaller neap tides. It shows the sunlit side of the moon on the left when viewed in the northern hemisphere. It rises very early in the morning, and sets around midday.

Much like the first quarter moon period, fish will feed throughout this period, but you will notice a sudden increase in bites just after the moon sets, and just before it rises again. As before, it is to do with moonlight entering the sea during clear skies, but also gravitational influences.

INBETWEEN MOON PHASES

Between new moon and the first quarter there is the waxing crescent moon. This is when the moon starts to become visible again on the right side. From first quarter to full moon, the mid-position moon is the waxing gibbous moon as the visible portion of the moon increases. In between the full moon and the last quarter moon, the mid period is referred to as the waning gibbous moon as we see the moon's surface visible to us on the left side decline, and between the last quarter and new moon the period is called the waning crescent moon as the moon becomes closer to the sun as each days passes and less of the moon remains visible.

When fishing these periods stick to the optimum times of low and high water and fish during the dark hours when shore fishing for the best results.

90-MINUTE PEAK BITE TIME WINDOWS

Data taken from all around the world shows that in addition to the general feeding times, and the peak periods, there are specific short windows when fish feeding activity increases dramatically. These periods occur for

45 minutes either side of the specific moon rise and set time.

The act of the moon rising and setting triggers the movement of baitfish shoals, up and down, in the water column. Bigger predatory fish respond to these periods and will often take 80 per cent of their daily intake in these short feeding spells.

These peak feeding times also occur when the sun rises and sets. Again we go back to anglers, and hunters, saying the best time to fish and hunt are dusk and dawn.

However, if you compare the differences in feeding activity between the sun rise and set, and the moon rise and set, then the moon invariably produces the very best feeding response in fish. If you aim to fish either side of the rise and set times of both the new and full moons, then according to worldwide data you are fishing at the optimum moment when fish are most likely to feed.

PEAK FISHING DAYS

There are peak fishing days too. This will be no surprise to anglers, but there is a definite increase in fish activity during the three days up to and including the biggest tides of each individual rising tide cycle. Once the tides peak and start to fall, the general feeding pattern lessens and catches reduce. This is thought to be due to gravitational influences as well as declining tidal power and shift.

To pinpoint the optimum time even more, the very best fishing will be on the day the moon cycle peaks, such as the specific days that the new moon and full moon are predicted to fall on. Again, evidence shows that this specific day has a habit of throwing up very big fish. This is possibly because they have been drawn in by improving feeding opportunities over the preceding few days and are making the most of things prior to the decline setting in as the tides decrease.

There is too much evidence worldwide to dismiss the connection between fish feeding activity and the moon phase. However, we are still learning about how this actually works.

Applying what we do know about moon phases, over time, will help you increase your catches, but it is a guideline to be used alongside the other important factors such as wind direction, low and high tide, ebb and flood, weather, water clarity, cloud cover, available food supply, venue, and all the other factors that need to come together to make up that day of dreams.

Chapter 5:
Anatomy Of A
Surf Beach

To the uneducated eye, a clean sand surf beach may look barren and uninviting to fish. Rarely, though, is the area of sand totally devoid of any feature. Having the ability to identify specific ground feature on a surf beach is the key to taking consistent catches of fish. This is watercraft, and it's one of the most neglected skills of sea angling, but is essential to learn if you want to be successful.

Sea fish are rarely evenly spread along the full length of a clean sand surf beach. Areas of flat, featureless sand hold little or no food. Casting a bait on to this barren ground will result in only the occasional fish being caught that happens to be passing through on its way somewhere else.

The first thing we need to do is get the full perspective of the beach we intend to fish. There is no better time than when the biggest spring tides fall. Try to time this so that the wind is off the land and pushing the ebbing sea, just prior to low water, as far out as it can possibly go. This exposes the maximum amount of ground to the eye. The second step is to try and get some height from which to view the beach using sand dunes or, better still, roads along cliffs or hillsides that adjoin the ends of the beach and overlook the whole area. Gaining height will let you see feature you are unlikely to be able to see when stood at beach level.

It's worth taking photos on your mobile phone, or, ideally, a compact or SLR-type camera, so that you have the opportunity when at home to further study the geography of the beach in finer detail on a computer screen. It also allows you to keep a permanent record of how the beach changes in different weather patterns. Over time, you can learn a lot from this.

SHALLOW CLEAN SAND SURF BEACHES

Very shallow, clean sand beaches tend to be lee beaches, or at least have some degree of shelter from the prevailing winds. Surf action is lessened on them and food is less easy for fish to find. That said, these beaches can often carry lugworm beds towards the low and mid tide lines that will encourage fish in to feed.

Using the height, when viewing very flat sandy surf beaches with no obvious physical feature, look for wet areas. Patches where standing water sits, even though the tide has long since receded, tell you there is a depression here, and as the flood tide moves in any waterborne food carried by the tide will fall in to this depression and hold there. This is a collection point for fish. In my experience I've never seen a beach so flat it did not have some depressed feature somewhere in its makeup.

Another feature to look for is where flat sand changes to rippled ridges of sand. This is where water currents tracking back and forth over the beach form shallow ridges. These will only be a couple of inches high, but this indicates water movement and food will get flushed out from the sand here, or get trapped in the ripples and ridges as the tide floods in and surf tables wash over the sand.

The most important area on these relatively featureless beaches is the low water mark. Rarely does the sand make a flat transition in to the water. Typically, there will be an incline in to the water where the average low tide line occurs. This is caused by wave action over low water, the time when the tide has little in-and-out movement, therefore more time to dig away the sand. This may not be a deep feature, but it will be a definite incline in to the water. Often this incline eases out on to rippled sand below low tide line. All along this low water ridge, and the rippled sand beyond, is a good spot to cast as fish will work along this as the new tides

starts to push. Naturally any food brought in off the rippled sand beyond the low water line will collect at the base of this incline and the fish will work it thoroughly. Keep casting to this incline, and just beyond it, as long as you can until the pushing tide puts it out of reach.

As the tide pushes you back, concentrate on the sandy depressions that held static water. These will fish as the tide floods in. Even though the water may be only a few inches deep, flounder will move in to these areas, and as the water depth increases, these will also be visited by round fish, such as bass and whiting.

If the sand depressions are still within casting distance over high water, they will continue to fish. If they are not, then catches on these ultra-shallow beaches tend to be slow at best over high water as there is little of interest to hold the fish. The exception may be flounder and school bass right in the edge of the surf. The ebb tide is also likely to be poor, until you come within casting range of the low water incline again.

These beaches always tend to fish best at night. Daylight catches, due to the shallow nature of these beaches, are rarely great. The exception may be when the water is coloured and dirty after a gale. The light levels entering the water in these conditions are subdued and it encourages fish in the surf to feed. In clear water they are reluctant to swim in water less than a few feet deep by day from a safety aspect.

STORM BEACHES

Storm beaches are also shallow, but they will face directly in to the oncoming prevailing winds and the open sea. This sees a much greater level of wave action and sea swell. This water movement is crucial to exposing food forms to hunting fish. Rarely do these beaches carry much static life between the average low tide and high tide marks. However, the low tide mark below the average low tide line will often see black lug beds, razorfish beds, and be alive with other food items such as white ragworm, crabs, shrimps and sandeels.

Again look for height that allows you to see the full perspective of the beach, with the bigger spring tide low water periods being the time to look.

These beaches are often flanked by rocky cliffs, headlands, or boulder-strewn ground at one or both ends. The junction where the rocks meet sand, especially towards low water, is a great spot to target bass, plaice, rays, and many other species. The bass will work along the edge of the rocks, and amongst them, looking for crabs and small fish. The rays and plaice are more stationary and out further in deep water waiting for passing food as the tide floods in. If a beach has little obvious feature elsewhere, the ends of the beach will be the hotspots.

The reality is that most beaches have some feature. The obvious one is, as on the shallow lee beaches, a bank of rising sand running along the low water line. As the tide starts to flood back in, fish moving in with the tide will work along the lower edge of this where food pushed in by the tide collects. This area can fish well for as long as you can cast to it.

Often, below this low tide incline, the sand becomes heavily rippled. Fish scour these ripples as waterborne food gets trapped here. Longer casts at low water can often find rays, especially thornbacks and small-eyed ray, quartering this rippled ground.

Also look to see if there are deeper pools that cut in from the natural low water line. As the tide floods these are natural food collection areas where food pushed inwards by the tide drops and holds. These spots again will fish for as long as you can cast to them with bass, cod, flounder, rays and turbot amongst the fish, which move in to these areas to feed.

When we reach the middle beach ground, observe how the sand rises from the low water line. Usually there is a gentle shallowing of the sand. Look for any areas where the sand rises steeper, or is dished out slightly. This is where a current deflects off the banks. This current will bring food in to this area, and fish.

The obvious and best fishing features to look for are gutters or deeper channels that run parallel along the length of the beach, or in shorter sections at an angle. These are created by tidal currents flowing across the beach. As the tide floods over flat sand and in to these channels, again food gets washed in to them, then is carried slowly through the channel by the tide. Flounder, bass, and, when deep enough, rays and plaice will all move in to these and feed. Even better if these channels flow outwards all the way to the low water line. As the new tide starts to flood, fish travel upwards in with the tide, through these channels, physically hunting for food. Winter cod, also bass and flounder, are typical examples of this.

Equally good spots are where a sandbank is split, right and left, by a narrow channel leading in from the open sea. Fish use this as a gateway and baits dropped here are highly likely to be eaten. It is a prime ambush point!

Also note any areas where depressions are formed by the tide. These shallow sink holes will trap food as it gets borne along by the tide. Fish visit these as they hunt, and flatfish will lay up in these as the tide floods inwards.

Also pick out any areas where a series of smaller pools show, holding water when the tide has retreated away from them. These will hold fish as the tide deepens over them on the next flood tide. These are often the home of sandeels, plus these will again hold food that gets deposited there. Note where sand changes to fine or heavier shingle. Rays and plaice, also turbot, do seem to like to lay on the junction of these two types of ground when resident on storm beaches.

The visually obvious feeding areas are patches of boulders, or where small rocks occur. Areas of rocks will be home to small crabs, shannies,

prawns *etc*, and fish always work over or close to these when hunting. Big rocks funnel the tide and this forms scooped out deeper areas around their base, and these, too, become food holders which fish will search through, bass and cod especially.

Casting directly in to or just uptide of weed beds puts your bait where fish expect to find crabs, small fish and other life forms. Fish will fully quarter such an area in a methodical manner and sooner or later will come across the scent from your bait.

Either side of high water, the option remains that you may still be able to cast to the middle ground feature. Experienced anglers like to fish two rods, one at range in to the middle ground, and one at close range. High water feature may be shallow gutters, gullies and depressions in the sand, which the tide, or undertow, has scooped out. These are good spots for whiting, flounder and turbot, also bass.

Surf beaches may also have sections of wooden groynes, or stone groynes running out seaward from the high water line. These are designed to hold the shingle and sand more stable. In my experience, fish seem reluctant to come inside the gaps between the groynes if these are only 75 yards or so apart. If the gap is greater, then there's more chance of fish moving inside these gaps. The ends of the groynes, though, will affect the tide running round them. This often causes deep holes to be scoured out of the sand around the ends of the groynes. These are excellent holding spots for food, with fish such as cod, bass, flounder, dabs, sole and coalfish all likely to be caught here.

These groynes also tend to see a build-up of sand on the dominant flood tide side, but with a deep edge on the leeward side. The deeper leeward edge is a good spot for flatfish to sit either side of high tide.

Due to concerns over sea defences and coastal erosion, many beaches are now seeing miniature stone breakwaters or groynes placed at strategic points along the beach to deflect the tide and reduce its erosional effect on the high tide mark. These are also great spots to fish up against. On the flood tide, try to fish the side facing directly in to the tide. This is where most of the food will lodge and the fish hunt. This also applies to the forward seaward-facing edge or end of the breakwater. The very best spot, though, is the downtide edge of the breakwater, as here there will be a pronounced hole scoured out of the sand and again this holds any food washed in by the surf and wave action. This is a prime spot for bass, but also cod if the water is deep enough. Flatfish, such as flounder, dabs, plaice and sole, will also visit this food hotspot.

Sometimes you get scoured out areas at both side ends of a breakwater, but more often than not (and this applies to wooden groynes too) the leeward edge away from the flood tide side is always the most scoured out due to getting the full force of the passing tide current at the very end of the groyne or breakwater. It's likely on the ebb tide that the current will be further offshore and the effect of tidal current around the breakwaters end is much reduced.

Another good feature to explore is where a small stream or river flows out across the beach. But some thought is needed here. In normal conditions the flow of freshwater will be a draw to fish such as flounder, bass and coalfish that can happily stand a degree of low salinity when the salt content is lowered by freshwater influx. The actual mouth of the river where it accesses the surf, or just to the downtide side of it, would be fish hotspots.

However, when flood water is pouring down the river and entering the sea, especially if this is from mountains and is highly acidic water, it will push fish out and away from the river source. If you have to fish near a river outlet during heavy flood conditions, fish the uptide side of the river, or as far away from the river outflow as is practical.

OTHER MAN-MADE FEATURES

Not all small features are natural. Some beaches have individual man-made pipes running seawards. These are mostly encased in concrete, but some are just large round pipes buried in the sand. These are usually shallow structures with the tide simply flowing over them as tide height increases. The side the tide hits on the flood will carry the bulk of the food, and this will lodge around the base of the structure. In fact, at the base, sometimes, after heavy wave action, there will be a scoured-out trench running the length of the tube. Hunting round fish, like bass and cod, will work through this trench looking for deposited food, so bait deliberately washed in to this gully by using an unwired lead weight can catch a lot of fish. The downtide side of the pipe, if the pipe or structure is shallow,

can see food items washed over the structure fall in the area immediately downtide. This is a good spot for rays, flounder, plaice and dabs. Much like the groynes, the very end of the pipe or encasement will see a scoured-out hole that will again be a stop-off look-see point for passing fish.

Sometimes the buried end of the pipe will be marked by a single large stone surrounded by sand. Passing fish will work around the big stone looking for food, so casting baits close to this gives you a good chance of finding bonus fish. The sand in the vicinity of the stone, especially if the pipe still carries a flow of stream water, can often form a scoured-out hole. You will see this on big spring tides at low water. These are excellent spots to fish on the early flood tide and for as long as you cast to it, as all manner of fish, such as cod, bass, rays, flatfish, and whiting, will visit it.

Some beaches still carry old single wooden posts just vertically sticking up from the sand. These were used for tethering gill nets or set-lines in years gone by. Although only a post, even this structure in a desert of flat sand will pull fish in. The tides will dig the sand out around the base of the posts and leave a large scoured-out hole that will collect food that falls in. Such spots are especially good for flounder, and both bass and codling will work through them as the tide floods.

STEEP-TO BEACHES

The deeper steep-to beaches may not strip on to bare sand at all during the bigger spring tides. Often the tide rises and falls only to reveal a steep shingle bank, and maybe just the divide line between shingle and sand, or a short section of sand. Even on these beaches, there are ways you can identify unseen ground feature and tidal currents, and increase your catches.

If the water does not recede far down the beach as it goes out, once the tide returns, the depth at the high water line could be ten feet or more. The junction where the shingle meets the sand will be the hotspot here and a very short cast will often be the most productive, especially for coalfish, flounder, dabs, turbot, and whiting. Fish will always work this edge as food gets lodged here.

If there is no visual evidence of apparent ground feature towards the high water line, look for areas on the shingle or where sand dunes start where waterborne wood, plastic, and other rubbish collects in greater volumes than the rest of the beach. This indicates the exact spot where a tidal current washes ashore and highlights a food collection area below the high tide line.

Weed accumulations along the high tide line are also good indicators. Weed is usually evenly distributed, but places where tidal currents come ashore will see increased weed deposition. Remember, though, this can also be due to wind direction as well, as we saw in the previous chapter.

Also look at the surface of the sea. If specific areas look rougher with a greater surface chop, or offer a series of shorter waves, this indicates a sandbank or area of rougher ground. Remember the surface sign, due to tidal flow, will be downtide of the actual feature, so aim to cast above the surface indication so that your bait's scent is washing back in to the feature where the fish will be hunting.

Other spots to fish are where concrete or wooden groynes extend out from the high water line. The very ends of the groynes will normally form scooped out holes where food drops and these are great spots for flounder and sole. Also fishing on the uptide side of the groyne will see food washed inwards collect along this facing side. Allowing a bait to wash up against this groyne edge can be deadly for bass and big flounder.

Good watercraft is really common sense. The phrase 'think like a fish' comes to mind. If you walk your favourite beaches during the big tides, noting all the various features that will attract fish and put baits in to them, you will find your catch rate rapidly increases and blank days become few and far between.

STATE OF TIDE

The state of the tide, on many venues, can be critical to catching. We're talking generally now, but on many lee and surf beaches, the period just after low water as the new tide starts to flood can be a really good time, with fish, excited by the new tide, starting to work inshore and looking to feed as they go. Some systematically quarter the ground, these being the round fish like cod, bass and whiting. Others, such as flatfish and rays, move bit by bit, taking up a static stance for short periods and using their powers of scent and eyesight to locate food. This hot low water period lasts until about an hour and a half after low tide.

The tide flow picks up more speed through the middle hours of the flood, this being from two hours after low water to two hours before high water. The fish can become a little less eager to feed when the tide is flowing strongest. During the middle hours of the flood, it is also a case of the fish being more widespread, so naturally bites will be less frequent. This is not to say that fish will not feed through the middle flood tide, just that, on many marks, the fishing can ease back with bites harder to come by. This is a general observation, but fairly accurate for the majority of beaches.

A very good time is the two hours before high water to dead high water. This is when the water is obviously deeper and food pushed in and exposed by the tide has lodged in deeper gullies and at the base of shingle banks. This tends to concentrate the fish close to the shore line.

Sometimes the fish will stay on the feed for the first hour or so of the outgoing tide too, but once that hour is passed, the fish, conscious of the chance of getting cut off or stranded as the depth quickly shallows, push out quickly to safer deeper water.

The middle ebb on a lot of beaches tends to be a poor time, with bites much harder to come by. However, if feature such as a reef or a gully still has a good depth over it, and fish are dropping back in to this with the tide, or using it as an access route back out to sea, baits placed here can still pick up fair numbers of fish. This also applies on the flanks of estuaries adjacent to beaches where fish coming out of the estuary after feeding have to work back over such feature as they push out to deeper water.

Chapter 6:
Estuaries

The coast of Britain and Ireland is riddled with small estuaries. These may be only 100 yards wide in places, while others maybe a half mile wide, but all are classified as small. They are, though, full of fish, and present the angler with an opportunity to enjoy some varied fishing for a wide range of species.

To get the best from these small estuaries, we need to understand how the fish move through them, and, more importantly, where the different species are likely to take up station and feed.

THE BAR

The smaller estuaries have what is called a 'bar', a ridge of sand that marks the line between the open sea and the beginning of the main estuary channel. At low water, you can often see this bar with surf running over it and then the calmer water of the main estuary channel inside. This is an important feature, as bass will shoal up on the seaward side of this just prior to a new flood tide starting.

All estuaries are different in their makeup and ground feature, but because of the fast tides that run through the main channel, many shallow estuary bars will see patches of seed mussel present and scattered patches of boulders and stony reef in the area just inside the bar. These will be fully quartered and searched by bass. These areas fish well to ledgered crab baits, but are also excellent spots to fish surface-popping and diving plugs over, especially at dusk and dawn.

These mussel patches will also see plaice present, taking up station on the edges of the mussel beds where they meet sand. The plaice move on to the seed mussel to feed during the early flood, but as the tide flow increases in power, they will move off the seed mussel and sit in the lee of the mussel bed where the tide flow is deflected and lessened. In the early spring large dabs can also be found tight in on the sand adjacent to seed mussel beds. Weed beds are rare this close to the bar area as the tides tend to be too fast and the ground unstable being mainly sand.

A quick reference to sea trout. They can also be caught around the bar and on the sand banks either side of the bar, fishing ledgered mackerel strips or whole small sandeel. Make sure you use a very light lead and just let the bait swing round with the tide to give natural presentation. However, once they enter the main channel proper they travel fast with the aid of the tide and probably begin the transitional osmosis effect of changing from salt to freshwater living and cease to feed while this process is ongoing.

THE MAIN CHANNEL

The main channel may not be an actual defined channel. It may only be, at least close to the sea, an area of sand with a deeper basin forming what is the main route for the incoming tide to take. However, on the flood tide, the side that the tide hits will often be scoured out of sand, revealing areas of stone and boulder, sometimes small fingers of shallow, rocky reef, but on the lee side still be clean sand. On the incoming tide, the bulk of any bass will be working through the rougher ground and not concentrated in the main channel. On the ebb, they will tend to concentrate in the surf on the sandy side which is where the outgoing current hits the hardest. Some fish will still be in the rough ground, but

bass follow the tide's power for the most part, so leave the estuary in the faster tidal current.

If the main channel is clean sand, then the place to position baits is close in along the edge of the incline where the banks of the channel drop off to meet the flatter inner channel. Fish, such as bass, flounder, and (in winter) codling, work the edge of this incline looking for food. This is where the tide flow is less pronounced. In the middle channel, the tide flows strongly, and fish in this are usually traveling and will not stop to feed, intent on going elsewhere.

Estuaries often have a bottleneck where the main channel suddenly tightens. This has the effect of speeding up the flooding tide. This can produce a large scoured-out area, often 20 to 50 feet deep with a near-vertical incline on the seaward side, but rising more gently on the inward side. The lower seaward and inward incline are good spots for plaice and rays to sit, but the hole will also be the hunting ground for bass and also winter coalfish, whiting and codling. It is also the perfect spot for bass to trap sandeel up against a flowing tide current in the surface layers if there is a back eddy on the inside of the main flow adjacent to the estuary bank.

ESTURY BOTTLENECK SCOURED OUT HOLE

Tide Direction →

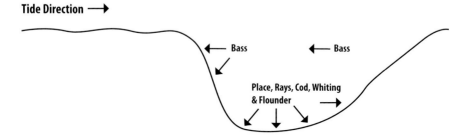

Sometimes the bottlenecked current will scour out an area of rock and boulders, forming an angled wall falling in to deep water. These are great areas to fish with lures for bass, or float fish sandeels through.

Where there is a big, wide sweeping bend in the channel, fish tend to concentrate here to intercept food carried downtide. The prime spot is on the immediate outside of the bend just where the current comes off the bend to carry on down channel. Food pushed on by the tide will collect at this point and then filter back in to the main channel. Bass will work this area thoroughly. However, for flatfish, fish the inside of the bend just in from where the current is deflected by the turn of the bend. Flounder sit on the facing incline of the inner bank right on the edge of the current and will either pick food off here or move in to the main channel from this point to feed.

FISH POSITION ON ESTUARY CHANNEL BEND

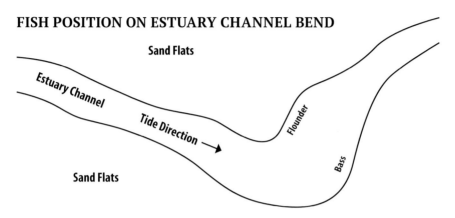

Estuaries tend to feature small harbours too, with a breakwater shielding the harbour and moorings from the worst of the prevailing weather. The main channel will splinter here with a side channel the boats use to access the harbour, and any additional moorings. This can be substantially deeper than the surrounding ground that will normally feature sand or mud banks either side of the channel. The inclines of the channel hold flounders, maybe plaice, but also bass, and (again in winter) codling, whiting and dabs.

If there is a protective breakwater, then this will also offer good fishing. The seaward side, when there is a good depth, will be affected

by seaborne swells and surf. This can be a good spot to target bass with ledgered crab, worm or whole squid. The swell and surf action will wash out crabs and also small fish that are hiding in the rocks that form the breakwater, making it easy feeding for the voracious bass.

The end of the breakwater will tend to concentrate the tide and create a tide rip when the tide is flowing strongest during the mid flow period. This is a good place to work a float-fished whole sandeel through, or, better still, work an artificial sandeel through the tide rip by casting uptide and letting the sandeel come round in an arc with line pressure, but kept moving with a slow retrieve. Also expect spring-to-summer garfish and spring-to-autumn mackerel to work through the tide rip with spinners and float-fished mackerel strips – the recognised methods to catch these.

The protected inside edge of a breakwater with its sheltered water can produce good catches of flounder that sit just on the edge of where the breakwater meets cleaner ground at its base. If the breakwater has a permanent depth of water, then wrasse of several species will live in the holes created by the breakwater, and along its base where it meets flatter ground. Again, living in the numerous holes will be conger eels too. Bass and cod work the base of the breakwater, as will huss if the water is deep. It's safe to say that baits placed along this divide line of stone and sand stand a high chance of being found and eaten by something.

Other good spots to try within the harbour confines are the harbour walls, fishing immediately down the sides again where the wall meets the seabed. Here you can expect all manner of smaller species such as goldsinny wrasse, rockcook wrasse, shannies, gobies, tompot blennies, sea scorpions, small codling, small coalfish, mullet and pollack, smelt, flounder, and if the harbour has permanent water all the time, maybe small gurnards and dabs. Also try under pontoons if they are accessible to anglers as these are ambush points for bass hunting the sandeel shoals, and you'll also see mullet under these using the pontoons as shade, but also feeding off the life forms that cling to the weed attached to the pontoons.

Also check out areas where there are multiple mooring buoys for boats. These use chains to keep them in place. In turn, the chains and ropes gather seed mussel and also act as a form of protection for smaller fish. This tends to pull in bigger fish, especially plaice, big flounder, rays if the estuary is deep enough, as well as bass, plus winter codling, coalfish and whiting.

Bass, flounder, plaice and rays will all sit in the shadow of moored boats during periods of bright sunlight and calm, clear water. It's simply

to get out of the direct light. It has to be said that fish in the shadow of boats are hard to tempt out to feed, but a dropping bait that falls right in front of them, or a moving bait pulled past them, or, in the case of bass, a lure worked to the side of the boat can be enough to trigger a response. Mullet also sometimes sit under boat hulls, picking food items off the underneath. A float-fished bait trotted down alongside the boat can again pick up bonus fish.

Some harbours have small jetties or wooden piers that the boats moor up to when visiting and loading. The wooden supports that punch in to the seabed will often have scoured out holes around their base and these are perfect for holding flatfish, but will also see bass, codling and coalfish check them out as they pass through. The supports also carry seed and adult mussel, and these can get damaged during the bigger tides and in bad weather, so again fish come in to check for this. Mullet will always work under jetties and piers around the supports, and take float-fished baits well in this situation as they have likely been weaned on to food being washed or thrown over the side of both commercial and private boats during cleaning.

As we progress deeper in to the main estuary, there may be small sandy or muddy beaches or coves along the edge. These hold a lot of food, such as worms, and will be visited by flounder as well as bass during the flooding

tide. The best ground is where the banks are covered with stones and boulders, sometimes interspaced with mud at low to mid tide height, but have bladder-rack weed along the high water line. This is the perfect habitat for crabs looking for shelter when they want to peel their old shells off. This is bass heaven, and every tide, some bass will work this ground fully.

The other hotspot to look for are short fingers of rock that jut out, either in to the main channel, or out from the high tide line. These will be fully investigated by bass looking for crabs on both the uptide and downtide side, but the downtide side, where the rock drops on to sand or mud, is the ideal ground to pick up a big flounder. Crab baits are rarely ignored for long if cast down the edges of the rocky finger on a flooding tide.

SIDE CREEKS AND MUDFLATS
The main channel will also splinter off in to side creeks, and eventually mud flats.

The mouths of muddy side creeks will not fish until they have a couple of feet of water in them. Fish, such as bass and mullet, wait until the current is actually flowing and pushing through the side creek, filling it quickly. Only when this happens, and the sides of the creeks become accessible to them, will they move in to feed. The edges of the side creeks may be small boulders and weed mixed in with mud, which are ideal for crabs and small fish to hide in. They can also be vertical or slightly angled muddy banks. If you look carefully you should see holes between the size of a golf ball and tennis ball dug in to the mud walls. These are tunnels that will hold crab waiting to peel their shell. The bass, eels and flounder come hunting these.

As the tide makes it further up the creek and nears the mud flats, the nature of the channel will narrow and become muddier. Here, in the bottom of the channel, there will be blow lugworm beds, also harbour rag, small white rag, cockles and small clams. This is a natural food source for the fish. Bass and flounder travel the main channel, and will access smaller side channels, but only when the depth is a few feet. Although this is a productive environment for fish, there is also a great danger of being found in a narrow and relatively shallow channel where herons often hunt. This is why the depth of water on the flood needs to exceed a couple of feet. Juvenile flounder may be present in static water all the time, but the bigger fish move in with the tide, then move out with the outgoing tide.

Mullet also frequent this upper side creek and drainage channel maze.

Their mode of feeding is to sift mud from the channel sides and muddy banks to extract small worms and small organisms. They will also sip food from scum lines that form on the surface of the flooding water.

Do bass, flounder and mullet ever move up on the mud flats themselves? Again, this is dependent on the depth of water present over the mud flat area. Typically, on the smaller neap tides, there is not enough depth to allow fish on to the mud flats and they will stay in the deeper channels. However, on the very big spring tides, flounder and (again if the depth allows) bass will work briefly on the upper mud flats. Rarely, though, does the fishing warrant serious effort when fishing these smaller estuaries.

Mullet are a different thing altogether, and they will forage and work the shallow mudflats, their V-wake clearly seen on the surface as they move. These fish can be caught fishing surface floating bread and sometimes single harbour ragworm, but rarely are these fish easy to educate in to taking the bait, or catch. In the deeper channels, they are a much easier proposition where the extra depth makes them a little less skittish.

ESTUARY TIDES

The best way to understand an estuary is to think of it like a motorway, expressway, or dual carriageway for fish. Fish are like humans: they look for a simple way to do things. The tide flow through an estuary allows fish, especially bass and mullet, to travel a long way without expending any real energy. It also allows them to feed over a large and diverse area, increasing their opportunity to find food.

Bass are the best exponents of using the estuarial tides to their travelling advantage. In small estuaries with a sand bar marking the divide line between the estuary and the sea proper, they will gather a short time before low water on the seaward side of the bar. As soon as the tide turns to flood, they feel it, and, providing there's enough water for them to pass over the bar, they will start to move in. While the tide flow is light for the first hour, some fish will work any ground feature within the bar area, but the majority use the gradually increasing tide to push on entering the main channel and moving far in to the estuary. They penetrate the furthest on the bigger spring tides using the faster flow and can show as far as the mix line where true freshwater meets the saltwater wedge and the river proper starts. There is some evidence memory plays a part here too, with some fish visiting the same productive ground each and every tide as they work through the estuary system.

On neap tides, with a slower flow rate, the fish will not travel as far and may only get as far as the middle estuary ground. Anglers that target bass in these upper waters all say that catches are best on the bigger tides towards the river junction, with smaller tides seeing fish caught lower down in to the estuary's middle ground. The bigger tides also push the saltwater wedge further inland and restrict the outflow of freshwater, which helps keep the salinity level more to the liking of the bass.

Mullet also use the incoming tide to travel far in to the estuary, again to the saltwater wedge and all ground in between, but again will not travel as far on the neap tides. They, too, seem to show a preference for visiting the same ground area over and over, but probably do not drop back as far as the bass do with the outgoing tide.

We'll now look in more detail at the best times to fish the estuary within a tide.

Low water inside the bar area, and in the main channel, can be a slow time for fish to feed. What excites them is when they feel the turn of the tide and the first surge as it begins to flood. This is the trigger for the bass to start working in towards the main channel in the first hour of the new flood. They tend to swim with the tide, covering ground quickly, but will also periodically pause and swing round to face the current if their sense of smell detects food. This allows them to follow that scent trail to the source. Once they reach the main channel and the faster flow of tide, they tend to keep going and will not pause in the fast flowing water even if they smell food. They push on to specific feeding areas, eager to be there as the tide exposes fresh ground to them.

At this same time, flounder will push out of the main channel and start to work in along the shallow edges of the main channel using the surf line as their focal point, feeding as they go. The flounder advance inwards until high water, then simply drop back with the receding tide, much as they do on the open beaches.

By the middle hours of the flood, the bass, and mullet, will have left the main channel, some entering or waiting around the entrance of side creeks, anticipating the deepening water. Others push on to feed along the small coves, muddy beaches and rock and weed margins further up the estuary. By high water, bass will be spread throughout the estuary system, but with the bulk of the fish within the middle and lower reaches and concentrated around the high tide mark. This tells us that the main channel is not the best place to fish as the fish are just passing through. The best ploy is to fish the early flood tide close to the outer bar, then move in to the inner estuary and fish the middle ground up to and over high water.

As soon as the tide turns to flow back seawards, the fish quickly drop back in to the main channel, again using the tidal flow to travel with ease and speed. Fishing down the ebb in the middle ground is rarely good. Again this applies to the main channel too. It's better to anticipate the outgoing fish and move back to the bar area and fish the edges of the surf line down the ebb, as the fish, once they leave the main channel, will work through the surf, feeding as they go, as they head back out to sea.

There are two ways to look at neap tides within an estuary environment. On the one hand, the smaller tides with their more limited flow of water make some marks, especially the bottlenecks and the narrow bends where the tide flow is more concentrated, easier to fish. This also applies to the main channel where fish passing by will be more inclined to turn and follow food scent back to source, though this is not an overly successful tactic. The amount of passing and floating weed is usually lessened on the smaller tides. Neaps will fish well for flounder, sometimes plaice, and will still show a few bass, but they are rarely as good as the spring tides.

The advantage of the bigger tides is that they flood much more ground to a suitable depth and expose a lot more food to fish willing to travel. On the neaps, the side creeks only fill so much. On the spring tides they fully flood and wash out on to the mud flats. The numbers of fish moving and willing to feed during the spring tides compared to neap tides is therefore proportionately higher. It's not a case of not fishing the smaller tides, but more a case of expecting the best catches to occur during the bigger tides.

Much like the beach, you'll find that the most productive tides for fishing within the estuary will be the tides falling four days before and up to the biggest tide of the cycle when the tides are increasing in size every day. Once the tides start to decrease in size after the biggest tide, the fishing becomes less consistent for all species.

THE EFFECTS OF FLOOD WATER

Many UK estuaries are fed by mountain or moorland streams and rivers. This makes them prone to flood water, much of which is acidic. Small amounts of rain have little effect, though fishing deep inside estuaries close to inflowing freshwater after recent rain should be avoided.

What kills the fishing in the middle and upper reaches is heavy flood water. The fish quickly move out, either going comatose in the deeper holes where the flow of flood water is lessened, or refusing to feed, as is the case with flounder and plaice, also winter whiting and codling. In the case of bass, they only enter the estuary within its very lower reaches not far from the bar area, or main channel mouth, where the salinity level remains acceptable, and the acidity value is weakened. They will not penetrate far up the estuary in flood water.

If the flush of fresh flood water is just a flash and passes quickly, fish will remain inside the middle estuary and wait for better conditions. If the flood is prolonged over several days or weeks, then the fish move out into more favourable waters as hunger takes over. It can take several days, sometimes a week or more, for an estuary to settle down after prolonged flooding and restock with fish to normal levels. After serious rain, especially in the winter, stick to the seaward end of the estuary and you'll maximise your catches.

DAYLIGHT AND DARKNESS

This is a personal observation based on nearly 60 years of fishing small estuaries, but daylight fishing can be hit and miss. If the water is very clear, then the chances of bass diminish. If there is some slight colour in the water, prospects improve. It's much the same when targeting flounder. Some colour in the water when fishing by day helps. This especially applies if the depth is less than six feet. Shallow water makes the fish nervous and reluctant to move out of the deeper main channel, or even enter the estuary at all as the bar area or channel mouth may be shallow.

If I have a choice, I try to choose a low tide that falls in darkness with, ideally, the full duration of the flood tide also falling in darkness. This guarantees the maximum number of fish coming in to the estuary, but also ensures that the fish will fully move out on to the shallower ground where the bulk of the food is.

The exception with daylight fishing is when there is a good surf pushing in on to the side of the estuary the tide is strongest on. In this case, on a flood tide, the fish will move in to this area and feed heavily, encouraged by the surf and the safety of the moving water reducing the clarity. Equally, on the ebb tide, they will also run the surf as they exit the estuary, feeding as they go. This scenario has seen, in the past, some of my best bass catches. It is the one situation I feel fully confident fishing in broad daylight.

Chapter 7:
How To Read Rough Ground Beaches

Clean, or mostly clean, sandy surf beaches, and even estuaries, are relatively easy to read, for, as we've seen, if you get some height you can instantly visually identify much of the mid and high tide features. Also, more is revealed along the low water line during the bigger spring tides when the ground is fully exposed. It is not so easy with rough ground beaches.

As before, it never hurts, when possible, to access high ground and view the beach fully from this angle, but rough ground beach feature is subtler and more minute in detail and structure, and this requires a far more methodical quartering of the ground on foot. This is the only way that hotspots and food holding areas will be fully identified.

Rough ground beaches also fall in to several different types with varied ground feature, and each requires a different approach.

MIXED ROUGH GROUND BEACHES
Mixed rough ground beaches are formed with a mix of clean sand interspaced with rocks and patches of shallow rubbly reef. Usually the rougher ground is more prevalent towards and below the low water mark.

As mentioned, if you can find some height above the beach, then do so. However, it is doubtful you will be able to identify much that will be of use from so far away. What may be visible at low water, especially in calm, clear seas, is the extent to which any rough ground pushes out seawards, but more importantly any fingers of rocky reef that jut out in a seawards direction, especially if they have clean sand either side of them. This is a common feature caused by tidal flow and surf action. If you can clearly see and note the position of these rock fingers and the direction of these as they work seawards, this is especially important.

Most beaches have some lateral tide flow: when facing west, it's typically left to right, and right to left when facing eastwards on flood tides. On ebbing tides, the opposite is true. Again this is a simplification, as other factors such as land formation can deflect and change the tidal

course, but that becomes obvious with time spent on a beach, and you can adapt the following information to the specific situation.

Due to this lateral tide flow, the junction of reef and cleaner ground facing the oncoming tide becomes a major collection area for any food washed along by the tide with the food getting trapped against the base of the reef. It is therefore a natural feeding route for fish advancing inwards with the tide to follow. These areas tend to fish best for the first two hours of the flood, providing there is enough depth of water for the fish to swim in comfortably. Such spots are prime for bass, but also flounder. For bass, two feet of depth, sometimes less, is enough, especially at night. If the depth is a good five feet or more, also expect winter codling, and with even more depth, say ten feet, bull huss and possibly tope will work this edge.

As the depth deepens and the rocky finger becomes submerged, and the tide flow also picks up speed, the fish on the uptide side of the reef will pass over the shallow reef ground and feed on the lee side or downtide side. The food that was getting washed up along the sides of the reef now washes over it and falls on the downtide side. This, during the middle flood period, becomes the target area to fish. Also, in very rough seas, the heavy wave action will wash food, such as crabs and small fish, out of their hidey-holes and see them fall in to the waiting mouths of fish anticipating exactly this. The fish move on to the lee side of the reef because the tide, being less here, means they expend less energy swimming against a fast-flowing current.

Although the uptide side of the reef is the prime spot, the downtide side can still produce a fish as the new tide floods in for the first two hours or so. The reason this does not fish as well, though, is that there is no natural deposition of food on this side during the lighter tide run.

HOW FISH FEED EITHER SIDE OF A SHALLOW REEF

Tide Direction ⟶

Low water
Bass, Cod,
Tope & Huss ↘

Bass, Cod, Tope
& Huss as water
deepens ↙

Fish working the uptide side of the reef are using mainly their sense of smell to locate dead food. The fish working the downtide side of the reef in this early stage of the tide tend to be vigorously hunting through the stones and reef ground trying to scare up small fish and crabs, whilst also keeping a careful vigil on the surface water above for small fish, such as sandeel, being washed over the reef. Although fish will not necessarily turn their noses up at any potential meal offered to them on either side of the reef, knowing how they feed suggests that the best place to fish baits is on the uptide side of the structure, and the better place to use plugs, spinners and artificial lures is on the downtide side. Always remember, try to present a fish with a food form it expects to be feeding on in a given area and you won't go far wrong.

If you spot breaks or gaps in the structure of the reef, or any deeper areas, and you can cast to these, then these are hotspots. The fish on the uptide side will use these to access the downtide side. Any baits positioned here will naturally intercept these fish, so make careful note of these.

It's best to take a landmark behind you and memorize this as to the exact position of the reef and its distance from where you intend to cast from. You can also visually locate the reef during the flooding tide. Look for calm water with a distinct rougher line of agitated water. This line of roughened water is created by the tide sweeping up and over the top of the reef. However, this distinct line will actually be a few feet or yards downtide of where the reef actually is. You need to cast just above or uptide of the demarcation line of calm and agitated water to be near the edge of the downtide side of the reef and inside the main take zone.

When faced with broken rough ground, round fish, like bass and cod, will sweep over the clean sand quite quickly. They tend to swim with the current, occasionally turning to face in to the current if they pick up any food scent. To get the best from these transitory areas, look for specific feature that will hold the fish. As when reading surf beaches, any gullies running parallel along the beach are good spots. Areas of scattered small stones may also hold a fish's attention briefly.

Better still are single big stones. If you look carefully at these, they mostly have a deeper depression around their base where the tide scours out the sand and often goes to bare stone and shingle. These depressions can be home to crabs and small fish like shannies that will take up residence under the protective rock. Bass know this and will fully circle the base of the rock, checking it out before moving on. Also, the depression will collect food again washed down by the tidal flow, making it a natural larder. The knack here is to cast a bait as close to the uptide side base of the rock as you can. This then sees the scent of the bait wash back in to the depression which will bring in a hunting fish.

Pay particular attention to larger areas of stone and rubbly ground set amongst mixed ground. Fish drop back on to these areas, will turn to face into the tide, then fully quarter the ground using mainly smell to locate any

food source, but also visually searching for the movement of small fish and crabs. They do this by letting the tide slowly drop them backwards while they face the tide head on and move side to side across the ground. It's much the same as a survey vessel systematically works across the seabed looking for anomalies such as wrecks. Basically the fish are searching the ground in a grid-like pattern. The observant amongst us may have seen a bass's tail fin suddenly appear waving on the surface in shallow water. This is a fish that has found food lodged under a stone or boulder and is grubbing it out. Bass are especially adept at this by using water sucked into and blown out of the mouth to flush food items out. Cod are also grubbing fish capable of digging buried food out of sand and shingle when quartering ground.

The same rule of 'find the feature' applies when fishing high water in to mixed ground. The rougher areas and heavier concentrations of stone and boulders will be where the fish are. If you have a beach where the rocky finger reefs come all the way in to the high water line, which is not that common, then, as before, fish the uptide side of the reef as the tide flow falls away towards high water slack.

This is where long distance casting ability also comes in play. If you can still cast to the middle ground feature as we described it, then you will enjoy consistent catches. On mixed ground beaches, typically the best fishing is from the low water and mid tide line. Fishing close in on to clean sand towards high tide will see you fishing to very few fish. Most stay out on the more productive mixed ground where the bulk of the food is.

SHALLOW ROUGH GROUND BEACHES

Shallow rough ground beaches can be classified, on average, as beaches with less than ten feet of water over them at any stage of tide. These, though, can often be the most productive, especially for bass and cod. These, and the heavy rough ground beaches, are the hardest to read.

High ground might help and, at least, in calm, clear seas, suggest where the rough ground extends to and highlight any clean sandy areas that need to be avoided. For the most part, this ground needs to be meticulously walked over during a few big spring tide low waters when the bulk of the ground is fully visible.

At low water, look for natural channels or routes the fish will follow the tide in through. These can be deeper gutters running inwards. Depth is actually not that important: if these gutters are just a foot or so deeper than the surrounding ground, it will be enough to see food washed along by the tide settle in to these by gravity. As we know, fish are aware of this

and use the gutters to penetrate deeper in to the beach as the tide floods in, feeding as they go.

Usually these gutters show themselves by holding some standing water after the tide has gone out. They may only be a few feet or yards wide, but they will concentrate the fish as the tide floods in. Again you may have to use a high tide landmark to line up the gutter, or better still use surface-showing feature, such as boulders and distinctive big stones, to position the whereabouts of the gutter. If you have a series of these surface-showing features leading shorewards, you can use these to walk back with the tide but still be casting in to the water-filled gutter. This results in maximum catches by having a bait in a confined area where a lot of fish naturally pass through.

Maybe it does take a more educated eye, but often, by looking down the beach, you will see an alternative route a fish may take. Using an imaginary eye, let's say that there is a depression in the rocks that holds standing water a few inches deep, then a few yards away a patch of rocks stands higher than the surrounding ground, and again maybe ten yards away is a single large rock with a depression in the ground scoured out around its base. This is what I call a natural run. Much like the game trails in the jungle or woods that a hunter instantly looks for to locate his prey,

features in close proximity to each other will reveal fish moving inwards from one to the other as the tide floods in. If you find one or two areas such as this in a wide area of otherwise shallow rough ground, then this is a fish's game trail and baits placed here are highly likely to be eaten.

Even beaches that appear to be just one continuum of flattish rough ground will still have areas that concentrate the food. These will be natural depressions or bowls, and they can be quite small in circumference, yet make the difference between success and failure. To identify these, again, during a spring tide low water period, walk the beach. Note any small areas, take a line up and mark off all the spots where standing water remains. These might only be the size of small fish ponds, or even smaller, but food washed forward by tidal force will drop in here and therefore will be visited by hunting fish.

I also like to get down on my hands and knees every 30 yards or so, and look seaward down the beach. The human eye is very perceptive and will reveal areas where the beach inclines a little more and gives slightly deeper water. These inclines work the same as the depressions, and food borne along by the tide will lodge here as it rolls off shallow ground. The tide flow, as it comes off the shallow ground, tends to dip downwards too, and often there will be a slight scouring action within the incline. This reveals small areas, sometimes only a few yards wide, of small groups of bigger boulders. These are prime spots for bass and cod to quarter around looking for small live fish, crabs and washed-in dead food. This can work in reverse by looking up the beach towards the high water line too. Not all beaches have a steady incline upwards. Some have a deeper gutter running near the high tide line where surf action washes out settling sediment, keeping the base rock exposed. Over high water, this is another hotspot and short casts will find the fish.

Areas where the boulders are bigger may give the downtide side a little shelter, and here small banks of weed can accumulate. Weed banks tend to be natural refuge areas for crabs, prawns and small fish. It's always worth casting tight to shallow beds of weed, as fish will visit these and nose through the stalks, trying to flush food out.

Big single rocks that stand out from the general ground composition will again be a target point for hunting fish. Even without a scoured-out area around their base, bass and cod especially have a fascination for these. They will fully quarter around them, but hedge your bets by casting to the uptide side of them. It's also worth noting that these single big rocks are also good spots to cast a surface-popping plug or diving plug, as well as spinners and artificial eels when a decent depth of water is around the rock. This is equally effective with a float-fished prawn allowed to float

down and fish around the very edge of the rock. This can be deadly for bass.

Some beaches have rock fissures at high water that push seawards. They may only be a few yards long, but the ends of these deflect the tide flow. The very end of the fissure on the downtide side will see a crease in the surface of agitated water where the edge of the tide flows. Just inside this an eddy of water is created. Sandeels, and food washed along the ground, will fall along this crease as it's washed around the end of the fissure. Bass and cod will work through the eddy, picking off any food deposited here. The same applies to any small rocky headlands that break the natural line of the beach. These, especially on the ends, will be hotspots for hunting fish. Again they are great places to work plugs and lures when the tide is running hard, and especially good to place a bait either side of high water as the tide flow starts to ease.

Although some fish will work the same feature as the tide ebbs outwards, rarely do beaches fish as well on the ebb as they do on the flood tide. However, longer casts out to the mid tide and low tide marks can still see good fish caught, though most fish, conscious of getting caught out and stranded by the receding tide, put some distance and deep water over them as soon as the tide starts to drop quickly after the first hour of the ebb.

HEAVY ROUGH GROUND BEACHES

These tend to be less easy to read and invariably have a good depth of water over them with much of the ground still covered by a depth of water even on the biggest spring tides. Their makeup is more fallen cliff, heavy kelp weed beds and scoured-out ground frequently washed by a heavy sea swell. High tackle loss is inevitable over this ground, and fish loss too, but this terrain can be some of the most rewarding, not just for the numbers of cod, bass, conger eels and huss, but also for the size of the fish.

Initially, it's back to basics, looking to gain some height to view the terrain from above during a period of big tides, and ideally calm and clear seas. The rough ground may look uniform and extend all ways without much that's obvious. What you're looking for are reefs showing on the surface that work seawards. As before, even in calmish seas, they will show as agitated surface water, often with a little white water breaking over them. Look for areas either side of them where the water calms. This signifies deeper water and is the place to cast.

Also look for deeper fissures that run in towards the mid tide line.

These you can often identify by looking for two distinct areas of agitated water with calmer water in between. These can be just a few feet wide, or many yards wide and snake through the rocks or be straight thoroughfares. Sometimes the bottom of these will be plain hard rock. Sometimes they can be filled with heavy kelp weed. It matters little, for these are again the routes the fish will work through and feed as they go. This is prime cod ground, but can also produce bass, conger eels, huss, wrasse, pollack and coalfish, depending on how you fish, either with baits or lures.

The knack to fishing these gutters is to plan ahead. You need to have dry points that allow you to cast in to the gully, and as it floods with water, hop from dry point to dry point as the tide advances. Often you only have time to have one short cast in to a specific section of a gully. There may be chance of just the one bite, then you need to move. This is where you fish light with a few spare rigs and weights in your pocket, your bait in a bag around your neck or waist, and that's it. Hold the rod all the time feeling for bites. I have to mention safety when doing this. Never fish alone, always with another, and only fish seas and marks that give you easy access off if the weather suddenly worsens. This obviously applies to all fishing.

Feature I really favour for cod and bass are where several big boulders, man height and the size of a car, are grouped together with deeper water in between. As the tide floods, these are real hotspots to drop a bait in to.

Aim for the sides of the boulders, or the deeper water between them.

Kelp weed beds are another perfect food holding place. It's obvious bass, cod, conger eels and huss will all nose through the centre of the weed, brushing through the kelp stalks and flushing food out, but this means you're casting in to the worst of the snags. Getting fish out through this weed can be very difficult. Sometimes you have no option and have to live with it. However, if you look carefully, kelp is often in clumps with clearer ground to the side. Where possible, learn the extent of the weed bed and aim to cast alongside it in to the clear holes. Fish will always skirt around the edges of weed beds looking for food that falls here, or gets washed in by the tide.

Another feature common to some beaches are rock fingers, sometimes called scars, that run roughly seawards for a short distance, sometimes only 30 yards, sometimes much further.

Often, below the low water line, the scar carries on seawards out in to deeper water. Casting off the ends of the scar, aiming to position baits to either side and in to deeper water, proves effective.

These scars can often be a series of scars much like the fingers on a man's hand and have deeper water in between, often full of kelp, but also full of fish too. You can walk out on to these and cast in to deep water, and as before work the gully back as the tide floods in. Often, and you have to learn this by experience, the gully will, at some point, have a junction of rock, or a distinct corner or cut in it. While the whole gully can produce fish, it's these natural breaks in the formation of the gully that will produce the most fish and are the places to concentrate on. This is prime cod country in winter, but also in the summer for what are called red rock cod. These being cod that choose to stay inshore over the summer feeding mostly on crab and taking on the red, brown and orange colour of the kelp weed they live in.

This applies to all gullies that carry mussel in them, but if you spend enough time watching the sea, you will learn that one side of the gully takes more of the sea swell than the other. A good tip is to fish the side of the gutter the sea swell is hitting the hardest. This is where mussel will get broken off the rocks and smashed as they roll around the bed of the gully, and fish will target these areas.

It might sound laborious, but I make a note, when fishing deep water marks such as scars or small headlands, of exactly where fish were caught. Over time, by doing this, you build up a mental library of exactly where the hotspots are that produce the bulk of the fish.

I've briefly mentioned it before, but it's important to fully emphasize that when fishing rough ground tackle, losses will be high. It's equally important to realise that the rough ground is where a large amount of food is consistently available to hungry fish. If you want to increase your catch rate immediately, then fish the rough ground and live with the tackle loss.

Chapter 8:
Rock Mark
Identification

Fishing open sea rock marks brings its own set of problems. Most marks will give good fishing for a large variety of species. Deep water, varied ground, a major and varied food supply, and, in comparison to most other terrain, minimal competition from other anglers who will be less willing to put the effort and time in to accessing these often distant marks, all give you increased opportunities. It might be great fishing, but there is no chance of seeing what the ground topography is as the water is way too deep, and the tide just goes up and down the rocks vertically, revealing nothing. We need a different strategy!

Nothing comes easy and the first hurdle to overcome is actually identifying rock marks that are sensibly accessible and safe to fish from, with quick access off from where you're fishing to safer higher ground should weather and sea conditions suddenly deteriorate while fishing.

My definition of a rough ground rock mark is one that has at least 30 feet of water, and preferably a depth over 50 feet. The ground feature will be totally rock with rising rock pinnacles, vertical rock walls, undulating rock fissures and deep water kelp beds. Inevitably there will be lobster and crab pots in front of you. It's a tackle grave yard, and all the better for it. Such information is valuable, but it is not on a fine enough scale to give us all we need to know. What it does is identify potential ground. The only way to fully realise the grounds potential and learn its formation is to fish it.

To identify potential rock marks, I begin by doing my homework. I choose an area I think could be good, then, using an Admiralty chart, read the ground feature and look for a wide range of depth within a relatively small area. I'm interested in ground that shallows and deepens dramatically. I'm not interested in flat, featureless ground, or ground that has minimal lift, or little of it. I then compare the Admiralty chart to a fine scale Ordnance Survey map of the area I'm interested in. I match the coastline configuration on the OS map to that of the chart adjacent to the ground I want to fish. The next step is to locate, on the OS map, footpaths that either run along the cliff tops, or feature very close by.

Now this is where I differ from many others. Inevitably, modern technology creeps in. Some anglers looking for accessible rock ledges use Google Earth to zoom in on the rocks and cliffs where they want to fish. Personally, I find you can still miss a lot relying on this. I prefer to physically walk the footpath, leaving my fishing tackle at home, just carrying my camera and the OS map. Having marked the exact areas on my OS map, by walking the paths and looking at the cliffs, you can often spot a way down that otherwise you'd miss. Even if it looks impossible, I will still go down cliffs and rocks as far as is possible with safety, and visually look. As an example, I fish two marks that you cannot see at all from the cliffs above. I've never seen trash or evidence of other anglers on these marks, simply because they haven't bothered to look closely enough for a way down and are totally unaware these marks exist.

Safety is my next priority. I'm looking for ways down that give access to a rock ledge or platform that is at least 15 feet above sea level. This gives you a margin for error should a rogue swell come in. Equally there must be access off to a safe area that puts you out of reach of any big incoming swell. I also need access down on at least one side to sea level in order to land big fish. And in very calm weather I may also want sea level access to fish close in with float or ledger tackle for wrasse, and spin for mackerel and pollack.

Another concern is where to park your car. I'm not averse to walking a mile or two to fish a good mark, but it also depends on the type of terrain you need to traverse and how physically hard it is to get there, and the limit on your fishing time that that can impose.

Our old friend height is not a problem when fishing rock marks as usually you're up on the top of a cliff a good way up from the sea. But with the depth we are looking for, there is little definition to be seen of what's below. It is true that often, what you are stood on and looking at around you, typically cliffs made up of cracks, flat platforms, angled inclines, up-jutting rocks and deep drop-offs, will continue on below the low water line. Any projections of rock or rocky fissures are typical structure that is predictable regards this. If these disappear in to the depths, then casting close to these at short to medium range will find fish such as wrasse and huss, maybe conger too. Also look at areas where the cliffs have collapsed and the avalanche of boulders you see may well be replicated underwater, as over eons there have been numerous collapses that now lie hidden below. Such areas are particularly good for conger eels. The thin, long

shape of the eel is perfect for lying hidden amongst the cracks in the boulders, waiting to ambush anything that swims by.

To gain further insight, we need to use elements we've touched on briefly before: the tide and the wind, and our powers of observation.

The tide is the most useful. Even in water 70 feet deep, natural underwater structure, such as rising rock pinnacles and vertical rock ledges, will show on the surface either as calmer water upwellings when deep, or as agitated water when shallow. You're looking for boils on the surface and areas where small waves are formed as the tide deflects off the hidden underwater structure. Remember these will be downtide of where the structures actually are, but make a mental note of them and when you're fishing you can cast out to the areas you think right and then judge, using your catches, as to exactly where best to fish.

Rising rock pinnacles tend to see huss, ling, cod and conger around their base, with pollack and coalfish just up off the seabed when the tide is running hard, and to roughly mid structure level during slack tide. Vertical walls are always good places to locate huss, but also conger eels, often big ones, that seem to like to sit at the base of the wall and pick off stray baitfish as they pass by. Shallower vertical walls, especially those right at your feet, are the home of ballan wrasse, who also like cutbacks in the rock that form narrow gullies that carry the sea swell.

TYPICAL UNDERWATER ROCK HOLE ROUGH GROUND

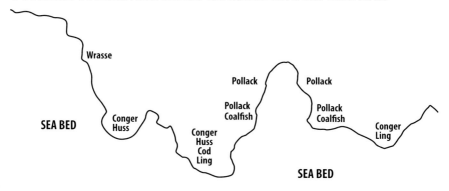

You find, when retrieving fish and tackle, areas where heavy kelp weed has accumulated. These naturally hold a lot of food, mainly small fish such as wrasse, pollack, pouting and poor cod. Bigger predators, such as conger eels, huss and ling will work through the base of the weed stalks, deliberately trying to flush out small prey. Baits cast in to the weed will be positioned in the perfect place for these bigger fish to find it. However, another good tactic to employ is to cast on the uptide side of the weed bed during a flowing tide. The tide flow will then distribute the scent through the full width of the weed bed and pull any fish in the middle outwards to find the source of the smell.

These weed beds are also prime spots for pollack to sit and wait for food fish passing by. The pollack tend to be right in the base of the weed during the strongest part of the flowing tide, but as the tide flow eases, they lift up higher in the water column and are more evenly distributed. They sit within the weed, sometimes just out of sight on the edge, but always looking down, in front, and above, scanning for movement and, when looking above, for silhouettes against the light-filled surface. Their powerful tail and body offers fast acceleration and they are adept at intercepting prey in this way. Working lures over the top and to the sides of the weed beds, then, is a technique that produces a lot of fish.

Inevitably when fishing rock ledges, some of the platforms you find will have small bays alongside them that penetrate a fair way back in to the cliff's base. These can be small, say just 75 yards or so in width, but sometimes much larger, with the mouth of the bay 200 or 300 yards across. Inside the bay, the tide flow is usually slow and subdued, the water less active. These are good spots for smaller fish. I wouldn't totally rule

these out as big fish areas, but generally any big fish caught here will be hunters like huss, maybe conger eels if food is in short supply, that work through the ground, looking to flush out prey fish, then move on. Fishing inside the bay tends to see you working to a small fish audience with little real chance of a bigger fish.

You are far more likely to catch bigger fish if you locate and identify where the tide current flows past the mouth of the bay. This will be governed by how far out any rock fingers or headlands stick out beyond the bay. If you fish just on the outside edge of a line drawn between the rocky headlands or fingers, this puts you in to territory where bigger fish will take up station and wait for smaller fish inside the bay to swim within range. Such spots are especially good for big conger, as well as huss and better sized ling. The tide flow line can often be seen as a definitive line of water that is more active and agitated with a definite ripple effect marking the tide, or sometimes a brown scum line or weed floating on the water will indicate where you need to cast. Inside the bay you will see the water is smoother and inactive.

The rocky fingers or small headlands that jut out in to the sea that form the extreme edges of the small bays tend to deflect the tide as it runs by. This will see a definite crease or demarcation line on the downtide side of the headland where the tide flows past. On the inside edge of the finger or headland, the water will be smooth and untroubled. The crease is a good spot to work deeper lures as pollack and coalfish will sit here, under and just to the immediate side of the main flow of tide, looking upwards and spotting small prey fish like sandeel being swept around the rocky point and struggling in the crease of fast flowing water. The immediate inside edge of the rock, where the water is calm, is a great spot to find big ballan wrasse right in under your feet and for some distance out too. Casting away from the rock, but along the inside edge of the tide crease, is where big conger will sit as food naturally comes to them pushed along by the tide, and huss will hunt here, as well as ling, and, in the right areas, cod also. Big ledgered fish baits or whole squid can be deadly positioned here.

Excellent marks to fish are where small rocky islands break the force of the tide, or channel the tide faster between the mainland rocks and a small island that is just 100 or 200 yards off the main shore. This channelling of the tide quickens its speed and carries food fish such as sandeel, mackerel and herring swimming in the mid water column with it concentrating their numbers. If you want to target fresh mackerel and sandeel for bait,

this is a top spot. This is also a feeding opportunity ideally suited to big pollack, sometimes coalfish, that will sit deep down where the tide flow is lessened, often sitting behind a rock pinnacle or ledge that helps break the flow of the tide and creates a slack eddy of water, then again ambush anything that is washed past them. Cod and ling will also sit here, but they will be hard on the bottom and pick off any small fish that is pushed deeper and missed by the pollack.

Most good rough ground rock marks will have lobster pots present. These offer both negative and positive points. The negatives are that they are inevitable and it's rare to find a mark these days without pots on them. Obviously they are an added hazard when trying to bring fish in from longer range with fish adept at pushing hard for the ropes and swimming round them. If this happens, then all you can do is give the fish slack line and hope it swims out of the twists. Sometimes they do, sometimes they don't. Live with it! Marked by floating buoys, the pots also will work left and right with the tide, and sometimes move out and back in again as the tide flow changes. Often the pots are on a long rope, so you need to judge this when casting and have an avenue of retrieve where you can bring fish in between the pots and rope.

Although often a real hindrance to your fishing, the pots do offer some benefit. To catch crabs and lobsters, the potter has to bait the pots. This is usually with mackerel, gurnard, pollack, or other high scent baits. When the potter has freshly baited his pots, which tend to be set in series as a long continual fleet, or sometimes individually but close together on close inshore rough ground, the fresh bait puts a lot of scent in the water. This will draw a number of big predators, such as conger, ling and huss, in to the area and close in to the pots. You'll be risking tackle and maybe a lost fish or two, but positioning your hook baits as close to where you think the baited pots are on the seabed can dramatically increase your catch ratio. Adjacent ground downtide from the pots, but still in the scent trail washing out from the pot bait is another good spot to be.

These open sea rock ledges will also be home to seals. The majority of anglers seem to dread a seal being present, feeling it is totally detrimental to the fishing by pushing any small fish out in to safer waters. I see things differently. In my experience, the presence of a seal indicates you have chosen your mark wisely and that there is a good stock of fish present on it. A seal is a far better fisherman than a rod-and-line man will ever be. They know when the fish will be there, and exactly when to fish for their best result. A seal is a good sign, and they usually move on pretty

quickly. However, on marks that are fished very regularly, you will find that some seals appear while you're fishing and will not move away. These seals have come to associate anglers with food and will rip fish off the hook while they are being retrieved. There is little that can be done about a seal showing this behaviour, though moving out of sight of the seal and not fishing for 15 minutes can see the seal give up and move on. Good luck with that one!

Equally good for fishing are rock platforms and ledges that fall directly on to clean sand, or a mix of mainly sand intermixed with a little broken ground. Though the identification and locating of these marks is the same as for the rough ground ones, understanding the seabed configuration is much more difficult.

Depth is unlikely to be as deep as on the rough ground marks. Typically, around the UK and Ireland, rock ledges giving on to sandy ground tend to fall in to depths between 15 feet and 40 feet. The tide run over sand is usually less than over rough ground sea beds, the scouring action of a fast tide keeping the rough ground always exposed. That said, the sand is rarely totally flat and will often be formed from shallow undulating ridges, or form shallow banks with flatter gutters in between. Both the ridges and the shallow sandbanks tend to form around headlands that deflect the tide. The enhanced tidal flow will shape the sand accordingly. The banks may be there all the time, but will deepen and flatten on the bigger tides and smaller tides as the tide flow speed increases and decreases. Undulating sand banks are good areas to find rays, such as blondes, spotted, thornbacks, and, in shallow water, small-eyed rays. Banks can also hold turbot, as well as plaice, dabs and gurnards.

If a tide run is very fast around a headland this can cut out a deep gutter in to the sand with a deep near-vertical side found on the shore side of the headland's end, and a shallower side on the offshore side. It's the offshore shallower incline of the gutter that tends to hold the rays as this is where the food gets pushed to by the flowing tide. The gutter will tend to be more pronounced on the downtide side of the headland in the direction the flood tide flows. Any gutter in the opposite direction created by the ebb tide will usually be less deep and contoured because the ebb tide flows longer than the flood, so the push of water is less fierce and destructive. This is not a 100 per cent rule, but is the most likely.

Sand can form a shape influenced by objects and formations some distance away, say a few hundred yards. These can be underwater reefs, areas of stone, rougher ground, and in areas well below where water is naturally channelled, such as between the shore and a small island or rock pinnacle. These tend to form as one rising bank with a shallowish angle on the tide side and a deeper angle on the downtide side. A look at the surface water during the flood tide will show you roughly where the location of this bank is by the turbulent water or ridge of small waves. Remember this will show a short distance below where the actual location of the bank is. If you reach such areas casting from a rock ledge, you will often enjoy good catches of rays, which will also move sides to face in to the tide over low water slack, but also see tope possible that come in hunting the small flatfish and whiting that live around these sandbanks.

Other good spots for rays, tope and huss, are where the mixed broken ground of sand and stone becomes clean. Rays like to sit on sand with some nearby rough ground to break the tide run and give them some protection. Small-eyed and spotted ray especially favour this feature. Big thornback ray will also sit on the edge of rougher ground, but prefer to be on an incline or angled bank of sand rather than just flat featureless ground. Blonde ray tend to be just off the rough ground and like a mix of sand and shale, or very fine sand mixed in with pebble.

These edges of rough ground that reconfigure on to clean sand can also fish well for red, grey and tub gurnard, codling, and for general ground fish such as dabs, whiting, and plaice. If you're fishing in the

deeper Scottish sea lochs, or off the coast of Donegal in Ireland from the rock ledges, then this demarcation line of rough ground on to clean sand is also good for haddock.

When fishing from a rock ledge on to known clean sand, do not make the mistake of casting to the same place and for the same distance each and every cast. When fishing a new mark, I like to fish two rods and fan the casts out in a half circle shape. Typically, I cast the right rod out to long range, with the left-hand rod at medium range covering with each cast an ever widening circle. I'll then swap over casting long to the left and short to the right. If you vary the distance over this wide arc, you'll find areas where there are sandbanks, gutters and uplifts. If you fish a plain lead and let the tidal pressure on the line pull the lead round, if it stops and will not move, it has found a depression, gutter or come to rest at the base of a sandbanks incline. This is a hotspot for fish. Take a land bearing behind you and note the rough distance cast, and repeat cast until you find it again.

To be a successful rock ledge angler, you need to fish the ground systematically, making mental notes where you get snagged, and especially where you catch the individual species, such as conger eels, huss, wrasse, cod and ling. This tactic has taught me to be able, on the marks I fish, to pick out and cast on to small areas of ground just a few yards in circumference that I know will produce a certain species. The spread of fish over rough ground is that predictable. Each species has its own ideal preference on exactly what it likes to hunt on, or take partial residency over. Learn these species hotspots over time and the return in fish caught is tenfold.

Chapter 9:
Breakwaters,
Piers and Jetties

Man-made structures, such as breakwaters, piers, and jetties, are natural fish-holding features. The shelter and protection they provide for smaller fish, shellfish, crabs, and variety of other marine life provides a permanent and productive food larder for all manner of fish, from flounders and dabs, to the bigger predatory fish such as bass, conger and cod.

To get the best fishing from these structures, it is necessary to understand how the tides work through these standings, how specific feature is created and forms between and below the structure, and how food is dispersed over the area of the structure.

BREAKWATERS

Breakwaters, as the name suggests, are protectors. They shield harbours, marinas, and vulnerable land from the direct force of the open sea. They may be formed in a straight line, or sometimes curved or angled within their overall length to suit the terrain and the area they are designed to protect. They need to be strong to withstand the force of nature and turbulent seas, so are usually made from large quarried boulders placed jigsaw fashion but with no natural fit, with concrete to form the standing areas.

When the stones are irregularly shaped and placed they leave large deep holes between adjoining boulders which provide a safe sanctuary for all manner of fish. Typically, conger eels will make a home in the holes that are on or very close to the seabed. They wait until some small fish passes by, then dart out and grab them. Putting fish baits tight in along the very edge of the breakwater's seabed structure, then, is the best way to catch these.

Crabs also take up refuge inside the holes, and bass will work their way through the base of the breakwater looking for them.

In the holes above the seabed you will find ballan wrasse, other small species of wrasse, and pollack, and occasionally a small flatfish that is rare on rod and line, the topknot. The wrasse feed on mussels and limpets that adorn the rock surfaces, plus pick off crabs and small fish. The pollack use the holes as a lair, and again dart out to intercept passing prey fish.

These can all be targeted by float fishing with crab, prawn or fish baits respectively. The float presents the bait over or across the hole entrance, pushed along by wave and tide action, giving a natural presentation, and again the fish shoot out to intercept. Float fishing adjacent to the boulders, but up in the water column, will also find mackerel and garfish.

Tidal action and the severity of the sea swell dictates how the ground feature around the breakwater forms. If the ground feature is predominately sandy, then sand will push up to the base of the breakwater and form an incline on the side the main flood tide hits, the more exposed side. This sees the natural holes between the rocks fill, to some extent, with sand and there will be fewer life forms living inside the rock cavities. However, bass, for instance, will patrol this edge as they know that heavy wave action will displace food hidden within the rocks and make for easy pickings. In calmer weather, flounder and plaice, and, if the water is deep enough, rays too, may work this same incline of sand.

If the water is deeper and wave action is constantly heavy on this seaward side, then the persistent scouring action and undertow of the waves will expose any bedrock and rough ground feature. If the ground is made up of heavy boulders and rock, and has a good depth of water, say over ten feet at low water on a big tide, then this is excellent holding ground for huss, but also for conger, pollack and wrasse. In winter it will also hold cod and coalfish.

As with the rock ledges, I like to walk a breakwater I'm new to during one of the bigger spring tides. Looking at the configuration at this time will highlight any shallow areas that dry out or expose as the tide recedes. This gives you the chance to note the type of ground feature and possibly how far the breakwater's foundations extend out until it borders the natural ground feature, be that rock or sand.

Very important is to also be there as the tide starts to flood strongly. Walk the breakwater and look for scum lines on the sea's surface, as these mark tidal currents as they push and deflect off the breakwater. Watch for floating debris, such as weed, on the surface and take note which direction it flows in. If you can pinpoint exactly where a tidal current hits a breakwater and deflects off it, then the ground immediately downtide of that mark as the tide flows will be a fish hotspot as food is pushed along by the tide and deposits at the base of the breakwater. Expect bass, cod and wrasse to be in the tide run, but on the inside of this deflection point where the tide flow is minimal or static, this can be a good spot for garfish and sometimes cruising mullet.

Also look out for lobster pots out from the breakwater. This tells us that there is rough ground here and baits cast to this will find conger, huss, cod, wrasse, pollack and coalfish. As already mentioned, when these are freshly baited, the scent in the water will draw predatory fish in to investigate, so fishing baits downtide of the buoy puts you right on the route searching fish will take.

The very end of the breakwater sticking out in to the sea is a hotspot in its own right. The tide hits this, then deflects outwards. As the tide pushes round the apex of the breakwater, this creates a crease in the water where the tide is moving fast on the outside, but is either eddying or virtually static on the inside. This is bass country!

The bass will work on the immediate inside of the crease and usually only a few feet down, working as a shoal, pushing shoals of sandeel and brit up against the edge of the faster flowing water. The small sandeel and prey fish, not having the power to swim against the faster wall of flowing tide, are trapped with nowhere to go. The bass can then simply pick them off one at a time. In deeper water, pollack will be in amongst the bass too. Working lures, such as artificial weighted sandeels or heavier spinners is deadly in this situation. Aim to cast at an angle in an uptide direction, let the lure come round until it's just downtide of you, then start to retrieve. This brings the lure through the edge of the faster tide in to the calmer water on the inside and presents the lure exactly as the predatory fish expect to see it.

In the period up to two hours or so after low water, and the two hours before high water as the tide flow eases, that same crease, though less easy to see, will also be a good spot for mackerel. Mackerel like some tide flow and will be up in the water column feeding. In the middle tide period when the flow is strongest, the mackerel will either move well downtide of the crease in to slower water, or be in the inside slack water adjacent to the crease.

This deflected tide will also scour out the seabed and deepen it on the outside of where the crease shows on the surface. Putting baits out into this deeper water either side of low and high water when the tide pull is minimal can produce consistent fishing for all manner of species. It's also an area of passage used by fish entering and exiting the area as they work the length of the breakwater on both sides.

Much depends on the severity of the tidal current passing round the end of the breakwater, but on the inside of the crease, and downtide some distance from the end of the breakwater where the tide current slows down, sandbanks can form, sometimes fine shingle and shell banks. If you can locate these, then these can be good for rays, especially thornbacks, undulate and small-eyed rays, also plaice. These tend to sit on the inner edge of the faster flowing current on the inclines of the bank and feed on the food brought to them. Mussel beds can also feature, and are good spots to try for plaice, as well as passing through fish such as bass and codling.

The inside of the breakwater is obviously sheltered from the worst of the sea conditions. It may be subject to some swell, but wave action is far more limited. This limits any scouring action of the seabed, so ground feature on the inside is normally sand, or muddy sand, maybe with the odd patch of mussel bed or light shingle where a tide current removes the fine sand. Feature to fish to is less obvious.

The holes along its base, created by the placed boulders forming the breakwater, will normally still be the home to conger eels, wrasse, smaller pollack, pouting and poor cod. But due to the lesser wave action there will be increased numbers of smaller species such as corkwing and goldsinny wrasse, tompot blennies, shannies, juvenile pollack and codling, and small gobies all living within the holes and along the edge of the boulders. Smelt should also be resident in season, but though hugging the feature, they will be up in the water column. Shoals of sandeel should also be seen swimming in the middle to upper layers. The growing band of species-hunting anglers can have a field day just fishing down the side of the boulders, or, better still, dropping small ragworm baits right in to the holes between the boulders.

Mullet are also a typical fish found working the inside of breakwaters in the slack water. They tend to patrol along the edge of the breakwater, pausing to sip food forms from either the surface, or the surface of the just-submerged rocks.

ANTICIPATED POSITION OF FISH ON A BREAKWATER

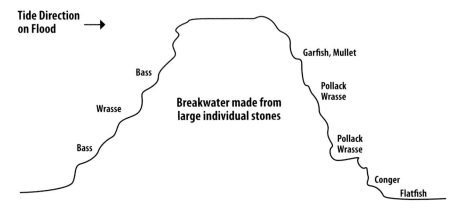

Being mostly used to create a safe haven inside a harbour, on the inside of the breakwater there will be a deeper channel that the boats run through to reach the quays or pontoons. This is a good spot to cast in to when the tide starts to flood through until high water as any fish moving in to the harbour are highly likely to use this natural motorway. Such channels are natural food stores too, collecting food washed in by the tide, but also home to many small food forms, such as crabs, shrimps and the like. The same applies to the ebbing tide as fish will again follow this to exit the harbour area. These are marked by channel navigation buoys, so are normally easy to spot.

Pay particular attention to areas where boats are moored within casting range. The mooring chains and ropes act as a protection for smaller species of fish and imitate a FAD, more commonly known as a 'fish aggregating device', and also gather food forms, such as seed mussel, on them. This, in turn, attracts bigger fish, so moorings are always a good spot to position a bait. Plaice in particular will often take up some form of permanent residence tight to mooring anchors and chain. Bass will also visit these looking for small prey fish.

If there is enough depth, say 20 feet or more, then mackerel can be caught right down the side of the breakwater on float tackle. Normally, though, you'll be casting away from the breakwater in to open water. Typically, the shoals of mackerel can often be seen scattering fry on the surface, so just cover the water fully and you'll find the fish. Garfish also work inside the slack water inside breakwaters. These also tend to show, either swimming in the upper surface column, or skittering across the water as they chase small prey. Float fishing works best for these using bubble floats, longer six-foot six-pound Fluorocarbon traces, size-6 hooks and small slivers of mackerel strip. Occasionally twitch the float and draw the float slowly towards you to attract the gars to take the bait.

If you spin or plug fish from a breakwater, though you may catch mackerel and garfish by casting away from the structure, it is far more effective to cast along the side of the structure and work the lures over the top of the boulders where bass, pollack and coalfish are likely to be found.

Not all breakwaters are made from loose, ill-fitting stone. Some are laid brick-like resulting in smooth sides. Again apply the principle of researching the ground on a spring tide low water and check what, if anything, is visible. Areas of rough ground tight in to the wall will be populated by all the wrasses, poor cod, pouting, pollack, codling, smaller conger eels and rockling. Dropping small baits tight in down the side of the wall will find several species, including the ballan, corkwing, goldsinny and rock cook wrasse, gobies, shannies, smelt, butterfish, juvenile codling, pollack and coalfish, with smelt higher up in the water column.

PIERS AND JETTIES

Generally speaking, we will combine piers and jetties as being the same. Typically, these are open structures featuring spaced-out leg supports, sometimes constructed from wood, otherwise from concrete.

Because the support legs are usually open, the tide has access to flow through the space between the legs. This always sees a deeper scoured-out gutter formed directly under the structure, often with deeper pools. This will normally run the full length of the pier and is caused by the running tide flowing around the leg supports which digs out the sand, often exposing the bed rock underneath. As the tide flows through and underneath the pier or jetty, any natural food borne along by the tide gets dropped in to this gutter and stays there. Providing there is enough water for fish to swim in inside the gutter, as soon as the tide starts to flood, fish move in to this to feed.

This is vital information. By choosing to cast well away from the pier or jetty, which most anglers naturally do, it is highly likely that you would be casting on to clean, featureless ground that will carry very few fish. The more experienced angler will choose to fish the side of the pier or jetty that the running tide is hitting. The tide will then wash the scent of your baits in to the scoured out gutter under the pier where all the fish are most likely to be feeding. When the tide turns to run in the opposite direction, swap sides to keep your bait scent flowing in to the middle of the gutter.

FISH UPTIDE OF THE JETTY TO DROP BAITS & SCENT IN THE GUTTER

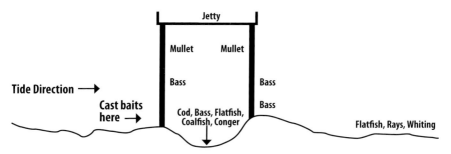

If the pier or jetty has larger concrete supports, these will deflect the tide far more than relatively slim wooden legs. As the tide flows around the legs, it will scour out much deeper holes. These are again hotspots where fish will congregate because any food washing down with the tide will fall in to these depressions and stay there. Putting a bait in to one of these pretty much guarantees you a fish.

As the depth of water increases, fish such as coalfish, garfish, mackerel and small pollack, also trigger fish, will work around the leg supports, which they use for protection. Using a float to fish a bait tight in around the supports is the best way to target these fish, with high water often the peak period when the depth is greatest.

Due to the flow of tide through the structure, the scouring action of the tide pushes any sand or fine shingle out to the sides of the gutter. This collects and forms an incline to higher sand a short distance away from the structure. These inclines are good holding ground for plaice, flounder, dabs, and, if the water is deep enough, sometimes rays. The edge of rough ground and sand is the natural runway for travelling fish to follow, for, as we've said many times already, this is where food pushed along by the tide collects.

Having concentrated on the gutter, it is, though, worth casting away from the pier or jetty to see if you can find areas where ground feature will hold fish. A good system is to cast in a wide arc at varying distances and note where you feel patches of rough ground as you retrieve, or simply find a specific spot that produces fish. This may be an unseen depression in the sand that flatfish choose to sit in, or a gully formed by a tide run that is deeper than the surrounding ground and holds food. Usually there are other anglers fishing piers and jetties, so watch where they are casting, and what they are catching, and use their time to increase your knowledge of what's in front of you, but hidden by the sea.

Piers and jetties are also built on top of rock promontories that offer a naturally solid foundation. This can see you casting in to heavy rough ground, either right under your feet, or more likely a little distance away. This ground can be excellent for conger eels, winter codling, and also bass which come in hunting for crabs and small prey fish.

Floating pontoons that allow boats to moor up against them are a common man-made feature that can be part of a jetty or pier. These give not just mooring options, but also direct access on and off boats. Often there will be restrictions to anglers using these, so you need to check if fishing is allowed. Some access pontoons do allow free foot passage, and, if so, they are excellent fish holding areas.

Because pontoons are being regularly walked on, the fish become accustomed to noise and vibration in the water, and, to some extent, human activity. Although it is important to not allow your shadow or a rod's shadow to fall on the water, which is a sure way to make fish bolt for better cover or go deep, noise, especially during the normal hours of daytime people movement (8am to 8pm), it is surprisingly a minimal problem. Fish expect noise and will happily carry on feeding, oblivious to what is going on above.

Pontoons are the perfect habitat for mullet. The mullet work underneath the pontoons, taking algae and fine weed off the mooring chains and the underneath of the pontoons just a couple of feet down and can usually be seen cruising around. However, they will drop deeper when feeding too, and can be caught on ledgered bread, especially if you hang fine mesh bags of liquefied white bread and mashed up mackerel on a short rope tied to one of the pontoons with the bag just dipping in the water. Also drop a few golf ball sized bits of bread straight down the edge of the pontoon to wean the fishing to taking bread off the bottom.

Bass are another fish associated with using floating pontoons as feeding stations. The bass are less obvious, tending to sit under the pontoons in the shadows, but will then dart out to attack shoals of passing sandeel, small prey fish and the like. This is where a fresh sandeel free-lined straight down underneath the pontoon during slack water, or, if there is a little tide, adding a couple of swan shot about three feet above the hook, will tempt them out.

Also try float fishing off pontoons for garfish, smelt and even mackerel if the depth is over 20 feet. Fishing the bottom with small hooks and baits adjacent to the bottom fixings will see many smaller species taken, including small wrasse, gobies, pouting, poor cod, shannies, whiting, small codling, sometimes juvenile gurnards, and much more. Estuary pontoons in the southwest and in southern Ireland can also produce gilthead bream.

Once we understand how fish use structure for protection from predators, but also how man-made structures create major food holding areas, it highlights just how negative blindly casting away from a pier, breakwater, or other man-made feature usually is. Fishing literally under your feet is far more effective.

Chapter 10: Right Rig Right Time

There are literally hundreds of different rigs available to the modern sea angler today, and each is designed to achieve something different. All too often, individual rigs get quoted as the best for a certain species, or for a specific type of fishing. Anglers also have favourite rigs and stick by them through good times and bad. The truth is that no rig is perfect all the time. To get the very best from the rigs we use, we need to understand the dynamics of a rig, and to identify exactly what we are trying to achieve with it. From that, we can deduce the best design for the situation we find ourselves in, given the weather, sea and tidal conditions prevalent at that specific time.

The most effective way to do this is to look at some of the more popular basic designs, then put them in to their best fishing situation for optimum catches. If you have an armoury of a few proven different rigs that cover most scenarios, then you can adopt those rigs, over time, to suit your own distinctive fishing. The reality is that you do not need that many different rig designs. What you need are rigs that are versatile and can be quickly chosen or adjusted to suit the conditions of the day. Although I use a lot of different rigs, maybe some 40 or more over the course of a year, the following rigs are the ones I use for the majority of my general fishing.

LINE STRENGTH FORMULA

Before we look at rigs in details, we need to get the basics right. The most important consideration with a rig, and a shock leader, is that it must be strong enough to take the pressure of the lead weight when power casting. The line used for the main rig body must be strong. There is a well-used and proven form table that instantly identifies the strength of line needed to cast specific weights. Simple enough, but vitally important from both a fishing, and a safety point.

Lead Weight	1 oz	2 oz	3 oz	4 oz	5 oz	6 oz
Line Breaking Strain	10 lb	20 lb	30 lb	40 lb	50/60 lb	60/80 lb

If you work to this table, using the appropriate rig body line by quoted breaking strain, the rig will be strong enough, providing you tie reliable knots.

The rig has to work in conjunction with a shock leader. The shock leader is attached to the main reel line and should wind around the reel spool eight times, run up the full length of the rod, and hang down from the rod tip about three feet. This is fine for simple overhead casting. However, if you are using a longer drop between the rod tip and the weight to increase casting power, the full length of the shock leader needs increasing by a further four feet, but still with the line wrapped a good eight times around the reel spool. With the rig attached to the end of the shock leader, and the line wrapped around the spool, the shock leader line takes the full pressure of a powerful cast protecting the weaker main line underneath. This applies to both fixed spool and multiplier reels. It's obvious that the rig body line needs to match at least the breaking strain of the shock leader for the strength ratio to be maintained.

Very powerful casters using high power casting styles, such as off-the-ground, or pendulum, will increase their shock leader and rig body strength from 50 to 60 pounds for 5-ounce weights, and from 60 to 80 pounds for 6-ounce weights in fishing situations. This gives an added margin for the increase and stress applied to the shock leader when full power casting.

The shock leader can be a straight length of the quoted breaking strain, or a commercially available tapered leader that goes from 15 or 20 pounds and is tied to the end of the main line, but increases in taper at the forward point to 60 or 80 pounds.

CORRECT RIG CRIMP CLOSURE

You'll see that on many of the rigs shown, rig crimps are used to secure the hook length attachment swivels securely on the rig body line. Getting the tension on the rig crimps correct is very important, for, if you over crush the crimps, it can damage the line underneath and severely weaken the whole rig when casting. To do it correctly you need a set of small needle-nosed pliers. Having placed the crimp on the line in the correct position, with the very ends of the needle nose pliers, pressure the crimp body until you feel it just close on the line underneath. If you want a crimp to slide slightly under heavy pressure, use one closing with the pliers in mid body. To fully secure the crimp and make it fixed, pressure the crimp three times, once near but not quite at each end of the crimp, then again in the middle.

RIG KNOTS

As for knots: as a quick reference, for shock leader to main line I use this simple-but-strong shock leader knot. If you need more strength, say when fishing in to heavy snags and rough ground, use two turns in the shock leader to form the granny knot, before passing the main line through it and then forming the Grinner knot.

SHOCK LEADER KNOT

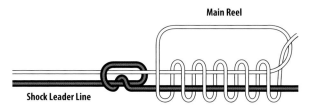

I also use a four- or five-turn Grinner knot, sometimes called a Uni knot, to attach all the clips, swivels and hook lengths. A simple, easy-to-tie knot in the dark and with cold wet hands that proves to be strong and reliable. It is also good when tying on lures, spinners and plugs.

GRINNER OR UNI KNOT

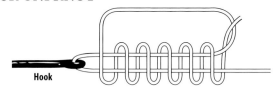

To form a sliding stop-knot, use a separate length of Powergum line, but alternatively a soft monofilament would be okay, and with this form a Grinner knot over the main rig body line and pull tight.

POWERGUM FIVE-TURN STOP KNOT

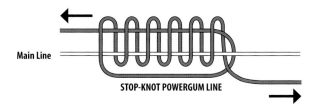

REVERSIBLE THREE-HOOK FLAPPER

The three-hook flapper is the most popular and, for the majority of situations, the most effective rig for general fishing when targeting a variety of smaller species from sandy surf beaches. In fact, this rig can catch pretty much anything it comes across during normal beach fishing.

It carries three individual hooks equally spread apart along the length of the rig. The total rig length can vary from just 36 inches or so, which is the common length when using shorter 10-inch hook lengths. However, it can be as long as 6 feet, or sometimes nearly as long as the rod when fishing continental style with rods up to 15 feet or more, to cover more ground by spacing the hook lengths further apart.

The advantage, immaterial of overall length, is that the hooks being spread along the length of the rig body create a wide scent trail that covers more ground and therefore has a better chance of finding fish that are individually scattered across the seabed. This is important when fish are few and far between and bites hard to get, but also when you want to target shoal fish, such as whiting, and you want multiple catches.

It is ideal for short, medium and longer range fishing in shallow to medium depth water, say at range up to a depth of 20 feet or so. In shallow water at medium to long range, all three of the hooks will be on the seabed due to the natural gravity bow and water pressure on the line. However, at shorter range, if the angle of the rod is near vertical and the line angle steep in to the water, then the top hook will be up off the seabed, the middle hook bouncing on and off the seabed, and the lower hook hard on the seabed.

Sometimes, having a sharp angle of line in to the water and getting the three hooks behaving differently works to your advantage. This might see you catching flatfish on the lower hook, a mix of flatfish and whiting on the middle hook, and whiting and coalfish on the top hook. The flatfish live tight on the seabed, so naturally favour a bait fished touching the sand. Whiting and coalfish are usually just up off the bottom and free swimming, so they happily take the baits presented up off the seabed a few inches. What often happens, though, is that the bottom hook catches the majority of fish, a few fall to the middle hook, and next to nothing to the top hook. In this case, you need to drop the angle of your rod to get all three baits fishing on the seabed.

The forte of the three-hook flapper, then, is fishing shallow, if you think about line angle, and medium to long range in medium depth water. This rig is not good for deep water situations such as breakwater or pier

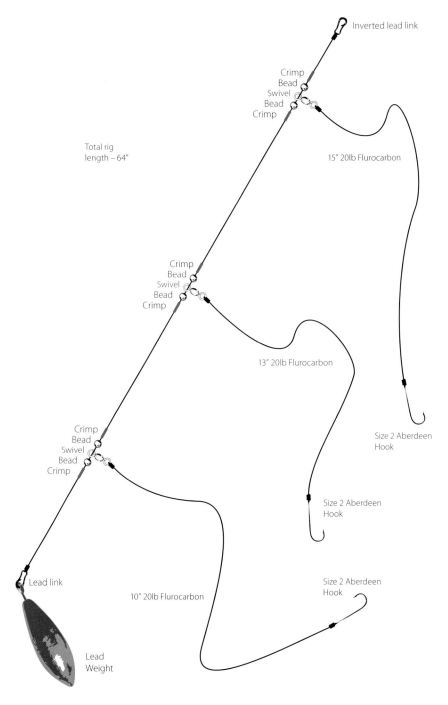

Inverted lead link

Crimp
Bead
Swivel
Bead
Crimp

Total rig
length – 64"

15" 20lb Flurocarbon

Crimp
Bead
Swivel
Bead
Crimp

13" 20lb Flurocarbon

Size 2 Aberdeen
Hook

Crimp
Bead
Swivel
Bead
Crimp

Size 2 Aberdeen
Hook

Lead link

10" 20lb Flurocarbon

Size 2 Aberdeen
Hook

Lead
Weight

fishing when you need to fish close to structure with a near vertical line. The majority of fish, as we've seen, will be in and around the base of the structure and mostly feeding on the seabed, or very close to it. The three-hook rig, then, would see only the lower hook fishing effectively, and maybe the middle hook catching the occasional fish, with the top hook pretty much useless. The same would apply from a deeper steep-to beach, though casting to long range would then see the baits more likely to be fishing on the seabed.

Most anglers fish a three-hook rig with the hook swivels fixed permanently in position on the rig body trapped between small beads and crimps. I prefer to use what I call a reversible flapper that adapts instantly to fish more effectively.

BUILD SEQUENCE
1. Start with about 64 inches of 60-pound clear mono.
2. Tie on a lead link at one end.
3. Slide on a rig crimp, a three-millimetre ovalised rig bead, a size 10 swivel, another rig bead and a crimp. Repeat this sequence to give you three full sets of crimps, beads and swivels. Leave these loose for now.
4. Complete the rig by tying on another lead link to the tag end of the rig body line.
5. The first hook trace swivel needs to be placed just one inch below the top lead link. The middle swivel should be positioned exactly 17 inches below the top swivel, and the third again 17 inches down from the middle hook trace swivel.
6. The top hook trace needs to be the longest at about 15 inches, the second hook trace measures 13 inches, and the bottom hook trace is the shortest at just 10 inches. All hook traces are made from 20- to 25-pound Fluorocarbon, and are finished with a size 2 Aberdeen pattern hook for general species.

A major feature with this particular rig is that the three hook snoods are positioned to present the baits differently to target specific species. If you fish the rig to a tight line direct to the rod tip, the lowest hook will be on the seabed, or at worst in a lively shallow surf, lifting up and down bouncing on the ground in a natural manner. With the middle and top hook baits fished just up off the seabed.

The hook snoods on this reversible rig are deliberately tied as different lengths. When fishing to a fairly tight line at close to medium range, the full length of the rig will not sit flat on the seabed. Only the lower hook length is fishing hard on the bottom and consistently catching fish. The other two hooks, if tied on too short a snood, are suspended up in the water column and less likely to catch.

This rig is tied using a longer top and middle snood. This helps to keep the baits tighter to, and in contact with, the seabed and inside the main fish-feeding zone, even when the rig body length is lifted by passing surf tables, without the need to fish a slightly slack line between rod tip and lead weight. The longer snoods also allow the baits to move more naturally.

By having a clip link at both ends of the rig body, you can literally reverse this rig around. If all the fish are falling to the bottom hook with the lower hook trace positioned well up above the lead, reverse the rig so that what was the top hook now fishes tight behind the lead. The middle hook is now positioned where the first one was before you reversed the rig around. This puts two hooks in the feeding zone, giving you the chance to double your catches. The adaptability of this rig makes it a 'must have' in your rig wallet.

TWO-HOOK CLIPPED UP RIG

This is the rig I prefer when needing to cast two baits to maximum range in both shallow and deeper water. It again targets a wide variety of smaller species, but is also capable of landing bigger fish, such as rays, should they take the small bait.

The rig incorporates bait clips on the rig body line. These are simply little clips that the hook is positioned in for casting, but when the lead weight hits the sea's surface after the cast, the rig body line falls slack, and the hooks simply fall out of the clips to fish normally.

The purpose of the clips is that during the cast they keep the rig streamlined, increasing casting distance by a measurable percentage. If we used the three-hook flapper rig, the unclipped flapping hook traces would seriously add air drag and noticeably reduce the distance cast. Reducing the number of hooks to two also lowers air drag and further increases the potential casting distance. Bait clips keep the hook baits neatly in the slip stream of more stable air behind the flying lead weight, which retains better bait presentation.

BUILD SEQUENCE

1. Take a 46-inch length of 60-pound rig body line. At one end tie on a lead link.
2. Slide on a rig crimp, followed by a three-millimetre rig bead, a size 10 rolling swivel, and another bead and crimp.
3. Above these, add another crimp, a rig bead and an inverted bait clip. The bait clip needs to be slid on to the rig body line upside down with the hook end of the clip facing upwards.
4. Slide on a rig crimp, followed by a three-millimetre rig bead, a size 10 rolling swivel, and another bead and crimp.
5. Slide on a crimp, bead and inverted bait clip. Leave all the above components free to slide on the rig body line for the moment.
6. Complete the main rig by adding a size 4 rolling swivel at the top.
7. Now crimp the first snood swivel in place one inch above the lead link. Leave enough room between the two crimps and beads for the swivel to freely turn.
8. The hook links need to be 20-pound Fluorocarbon between 12 and 18 inches long.
9. Slide on a five-millimetre rig bead to act as a bait stop, and tie on a size 2 Aberdeen hook.

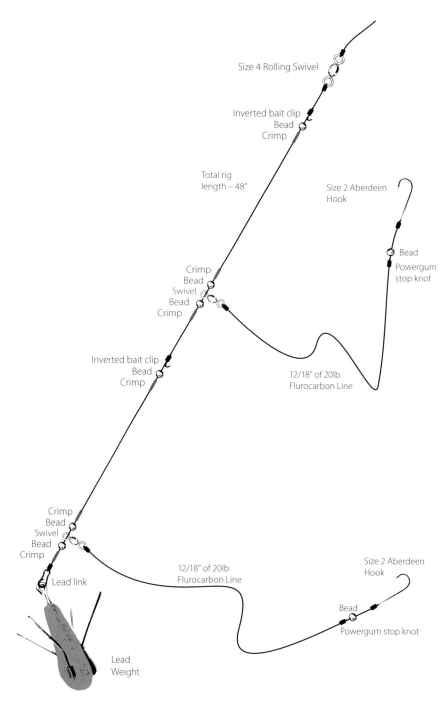

Size 4 Rolling Swivel

Inverted bait clip
Bead
Crimp

Total rig
length – 48"

Size 2 Aberdeen
Hook

Crimp
Bead
Swivel
Bead
Crimp

Bead
Powergum
stop knot

Inverted bait clip
Bead
Crimp

12/18" of 20lb
Flurocarbon Line

Crimp
Bead
Swivel
Bead
Crimp

Lead link

12/18" of 20lb
Flurocarbon Line

Size 2 Aberdeen
Hook

Bead

Powergum stop knot

Lead
Weight

10. Above the five-millimetre bead tie in a five-turn Powergum stop knot.
11. Position the hook in the bait clip and slide the bait clip up the rig until the hook snood comes just tight. Slide the crimp and bead up towards the bait clip and crimp it in place half an inch below the bait clip to allow the clip to slide a little under pressure.
12. The second snood swivel needs crimping about three inches above the first bait clip. Tie on the hook length, with the Powergum stop-knot, rig bead and hook added to finish.
13. Position the bait clip and crimp in place as before. This positions the top hook inside the bait clip just a couple of inches or so below the main size 4 connector swivel.

There is no real need for bait stops above the hook on this rig as the air pressure during the cast is forcing the bait towards the hook, but it helps give a neater bait presentation, and especially when using small delicate ragworm and lug baits.

Having the lowest hook link positioned tight behind the lead weight is the best presentation position when targeting flatfish, such as flounder, dabs and plaice, as the bait is kept tight to the seabed. The higher second hook, though remaining in the flatfish feeding zone, will have a little more movement in the tide and surf tables, and this tends to pick out round fish such as whiting, coalfish, bass and codling.

In calmer seas, the hook links can be lengthened up to 18 inches or more. This gives more natural movement to the baits. However, in rougher seas and when fishing in amongst the surf tables, shorter 12-inch hook snoods will tangle less and give feeding fish a more static target to hit.

Using two hooks means you can use different bait combinations to find out which fish species are present, but also allows you to experiment with different baits and bait combinations to ascertain which baits are most effective on the day to maximise your catch. Having two baits in close proximity also maximises the scent trail to pull fish in from further away.

Typically hook lengths need be no more than 25 pounds and typically 20 pounds is a good all-round choice. However, in clear, calm sea conditions, dropping down to just 10-pound Fluorocarbon and small size 6 Aberdeen hooks can increase the catch rate substantially when fishing at long range in shallow water.

THREE-HOOK Fluorocarbon GHOST RIG

This rig has proved immensely successful for me when fishing shallow, clean sand surf beaches in very clear water at any time of year, but especially in the period February through April when fish are few and far between inshore and often hard to tempt in difficult sea and weather conditions. It uses minimal components, hence the term 'ghost rig', making it less easy for shy, less-inclined-to-feed fish to see, plus it presents small baits delicately to give more natural movement. It will take most general inshore species at close to medium range, but is especially effective for flounders, dabs, plaice, whiting, small codling, rockling, small turbot and school bass.

BUILD SEQUENCE

1. Begin with 54 inches of 60-pound Fluorocarbon.
2. At one end, tie on a lead link
3. Slide on three large clear oval two-way beads.
4. To the free end of the Fluorocarbon, tie on a size 4 rolling swivel.
5. Either side of each bead, tie on to the rig body line a five-turn Grinner knot from 14-pound clear Powergum. Position one bead just below the top swivel, the second bead in the middle of the rig, and the bottom bead just above the lead link.
6. Using 50-pound Fluorocarbon, cut off three separate two-and-a-half-inch lengths.
7. Using a cigarette lighter, apply the flame to one end of the Fluorocarbon sections to form a bulb shape.
8. Slide one of the Fluorocarbon lengths in to the horizontal hole in each two-way bead, then, with the flame, bulb the remaining end.
9. Using a seven-turn Grinner knot, tie a section of 12-pound Fluorocarbon over the short section of the 50-pound Fluorocarbon and pull tight up to the bulb. The hook lengths need to be about 14 inches long.
10. Finish the hook traces with a fine wire Aberdeen hook size 6.

When rigging two-way oval beads normally, you either use a knot to lock the hook length line in the middle hole, or add a small bead, then knot the line, the bead then butting up to the two-way bead. This rig eliminates this and its potential knot and bead weakness. The flame-softened bulb in the Fluorocarbon sets hard and is strong. It butts up to the two-way bead and cannot pull through, even under heavy pressure. What is more, with the hook length being attached to the short section of Fluorocarbon, and the knot tucking in tightly behind the bulb, the hook length is as strong

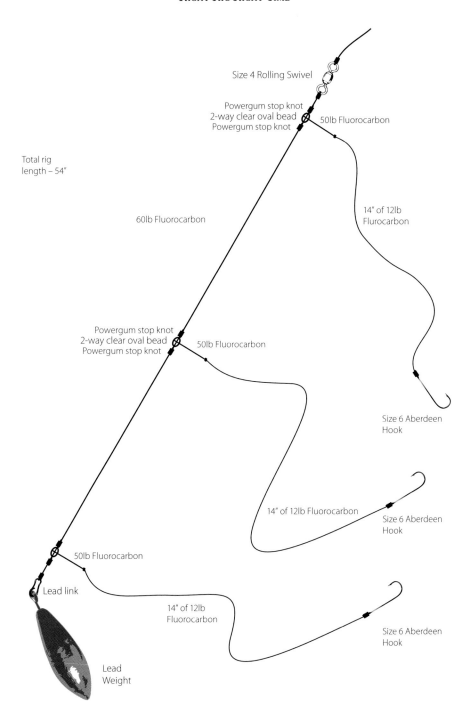

Size 4 Rolling Swivel

Powergum stop knot
2-way clear oval bead
Powergum stop knot

50lb Fluorocarbon

Total rig
length – 54"

60lb Fluorocarbon

14" of 12lb
Flurocarbon

Powergum stop knot
2-way clear oval bead
Powergum stop knot

50lb Fluorocarbon

Size 6 Aberdeen
Hook

14" of 12lb Fluorocarbon

Size 6 Aberdeen
Hook

50lb Fluorocarbon

Lead link

14" of 12lb
Fluorocarbon

Size 6 Aberdeen
Hook

Lead
Weight

as possible and capable of landing bigger sized fish without fear of knots pulling through the two-way bead.

Because of the bulb in the short section, the tying of very weak hook lengths, such as six-pound Fluorocarbon when targeting very small or very shy fish, is easier and stronger, plus the heavier 50-pound Fluorocarbon standing off from the rig body reduces the chances of tangles.

The sliding stop knots give you the option of repositioning the two-way beads closer to, or further away from the lead weight as conditions and bites dictate. A bigger fish may slide a bead down, but it is easily repositioned.

For close-quarter casting with lighter lead weights, you can streamline the rig even further by reducing the rig body line to 20- or 30-pound Fluorocarbon. Also switch to the smaller medium sized two-way beads. The middle hole retains the same diameter as the large sized two-way bead still allowing the use of the stiff 50-pound Fluorocarbon for the stand-off sections. However, the sections can be made shorter at two inches.

ONE-HOOK SLIDING PATERNOSTER

This is my first choice rig for bass fishing into rough ground with crab baits. It is designed for maximum bite detection. The sliding swivel is free to slide on the main line or leader, so the hook length and main line are pulling in exactly the same direction. The slightest pull by a fish on the hook end is transmitted straight through to the rod tip, giving maximum bite detection through the rod to your hands.

It is best fished with the rod held in the hands all the time to facilitate the quick striking of bites, but also with the rod horizontal across the angler's body to keep the line at a low angle entering the water, again for the maximum detection of any movement at the hook end.

BUILD SEQUENCE

1. Slide on to your main line or leader a size 6 rolling swivel.
2. Slide on a black five-millimetre bead.
3. Tie on a size 6 rolling swivel.
4. To the free eye on the sliding swivel, tie on 20 inches of 15- to 20-pound clear mono or Fluorocarbon. This takes the lead weight, usually one to two ounces, which is tied direct to main line with no link when rough ground fishing.
5. To the end of the swivel tie on 6 inches to 15 inches of 20-pound Fluorocarbon line.
6. Finish by tying to the hook trace a Viking pattern size 4/0.

You can make this rig even more sensitive by shortening the hook trace to between six and eight inches long. This means that as soon as a fish picks up the bait, you will be aware of it. However, in very calm seas, a longer hook trace may be necessary, anything up to 15 inches, if the fish are cautious and unsure when feeding in shallow clear water and you want the bait further away from the rig swivels and main line so as not to alert an already-spooked fish. This longer hook length also gives the fish more room to fully take the bait in, turn and move away downtide before coming up tight on the rod tip.

The rig, as described, is designed for close range casting using a maximum of 20-pound line from the sliding swivel, so that if the lead weight gets snagged in boulders or rocks the line to the lead will easily break when pulled. The main reel line would be 25 pound in this case, but no leader is needed as the weights will be two ounces or less and the casting distance is short, usually less than 40 yards.

If this rig is to be used for medium range casting with potentially weights up to five ounces, then the line between the sliding swivel and the weight needs to be 60 pounds. In this case you would also use a clear leader of 60 pounds on the end of the main reel line, which over sand only needs to be 15 pounds.

When fishing short range in relatively shallow clear water, it pays to use Fluorocarbon hook lengths and line section to the weight as opposed to normal monofilament line. It makes it harder for the eagle-eyed bass to spot the line, which may well be moving slightly in the tide.

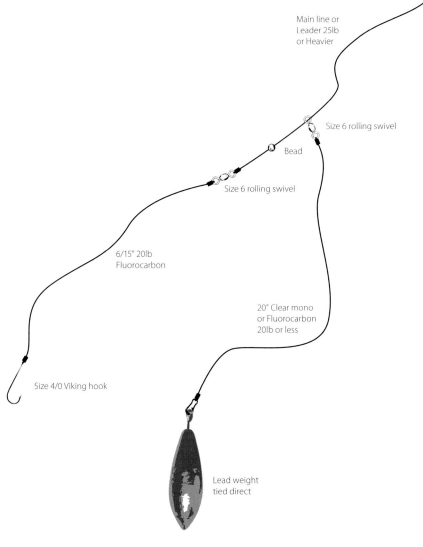

Main line or Leader 25lb or Heavier

Size 6 rolling swivel

Bead

Size 6 rolling swivel

6/15" 20lb Fluorocarbon

20" Clear mono or Fluorocarbon 20lb or less

Size 4/0 Viking hook

Lead weight tied direct

PULLEY RIG

A rig that I use for clean sand, and mixed broken ground fishing when targeting rays, cod, and bass. The rig gets its name because when a fish pulls on the hook, the lead weight slides backwards through the connector swivel exactly like a pulley system.

BUILD SEQUENCE

1. Begin with 60 inches of 60-pound clear mono.
2. At one end, tie on a bait/lead clip.
3. Slide on a five-millimetre rig bead, a pulley rig bead, and another five-millimetre rig bead.
4. Leaving a good 24 inches of free end to form the hook snood, tie in a figure-of-eight knot.
5. On the free end forming the hook length, slide on a five-millimetre rig bead.
6. Tie on a Viking or Aberdeen pattern hook size 3/0.
7. Above the bead positioned above the hook, tie on a Powergum sliding stop knot to act as a bait stop.

The key component with this rig is the pulley rig bead. This is designed to spread repeated casting pressure on the 60-pound mono rig body without weakening the line. If you prefer you can replace the pulley rig bead with a standard size 4 rolling swivel but this eventually creates a weakness in the rig body line after repeated casting due to the thin diameter of wire used to form the eye of the swivel. The swivel eye will naturally position itself on the same small section of rig body line for each and every cast. This area then stretches and contracts under casting load and eventually weakens, creating a crack off.

When ready to cast, position the baited hook into the angled leg on the clip link, and cast. As the weight and bait hit the seabed the bait will fall free and the hook trace straightens in the tide to give normal bait presentation.

The pulley effect has several advantages. Firstly, the weight of a fish pulling on the rig breaks out the release wire lead from the seabed. This means the fish will invariably hook itself against the grip wires and the full weight of the lead weight when it lifts from the seabed usually ensures lip hooking and easy removal of the hook for catch and release.

The other big advantage is that when a sizeable fish is hooked, the rig body line slides through the swivel eye, pulling the weight upwards until it cannot travel further. This is an advantage when reeling in fish over

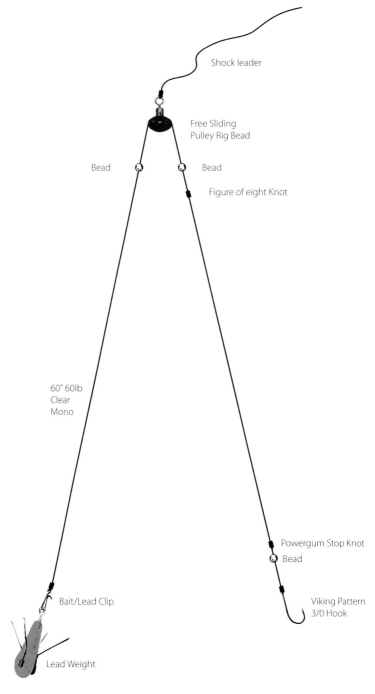

Shock leader

Free Sliding
Pulley Rig Bead

Bead

Bead

Figure of eight Knot

60" 60lb
Clear
Mono

Powergum Stop Knot

Bead

Viking Pattern
3/0 Hook

Bait/Lead Clip

Lead Weight

broken or rough ground that can snag the lead during the retrieve as the weight is returned held up in the water well away from potential snags.

Equally advantageous is that, with this rig, being made from a single length of 60-pound mono, when a fish pulls the weight up to the swivel you have the maximum length of heavy trace between the fish and the rig swivel. This length of 60-pound mono acts like a rubbing leader should the fish and trace come in to contact during the fight. The 60-pound mono being so tough can also take minor abrasion when bringing fish back across rougher ground, but also a big fish can be held initially in the water and then landed using an incoming wave holding the strong hook trace.

The five-millimetre bead and Powergum stop knot are vitally important too. These should be positioned tight above the bait after presentation to stop the bait sliding up the hook trace during the cast due to air pressure. This maintains perfect presentation, even when long-range casting, and keeps the bait concentrated on the hook. Without it the bait can slide upwards and off the hook on to the trace line. Fish will then try to eat the bait but miss the hook.

Many ray rigs will suggest using two hooks in line, called a 'Pennel' rig. The majority of experienced ray anglers prefer a single hook as even big rays have relatively small mouths. Rays are greedy feeders too, and if interested in a bait they will usually eat it without hesitation, therefore large baits are not needed. Small chunks of mackerel, herring or sandeel big enough to fill a 3/0 hook is enough.

ROUGH GROUND PULLEY RIG

This is the same basic principle as the pulley rig I use over clean sand, but for rough ground it incorporates stronger line to cope with the greater risk of wear and abrasion, and with added design features.

BUILD SEQUENCE

1. Begin with 80 inches of 80-pound clear mono. To one end of the 80-pound line, tie in a two-inch loop using a double granny knot. You'll see why shortly.
2. Above the granny knot add a bait clip, a five-millimetre bead, then leaving about 4 inches for the bait clip to slide in, tie in a figure-of-eight knot to form a stop.
3. Now slide on a bead, a pulley rig bead, another bead, then tie in a figure-of-eight knot to form the hook length, which should be slightly shorter than the length of the main rig body.
4. On to the hook length add an eight-millimetre bead, then tie on a 6/0 Viking pattern hook.
5. Above the bead on the hook trace tie on a five-turn stop-knot from 22-pound Powergum. This and the bead act as a bait stop to avoid the bait flying up the hook trace during the cast.

I make lead weights with a straight tail wire, then form a dogleg in the wire. I tie a short weak link of light line to the loop and to the lead's wire tail, then put the wire dogleg inside the loop for casting. This bounces out when the weight hits the water, leaving you just on the weak link of line. That said, any safe shop-bought weak link system works just as well, but these clip-like systems can jam in the rocks. The line loop doesn't.

This same pulley rig can be used for big conger eels in heavy rough ground too, but change the rig line for 150-pound mono. Big conger will take the rig through sharp rocks and can also bite their way through lighter mono, hence my preference for 150 pounds.

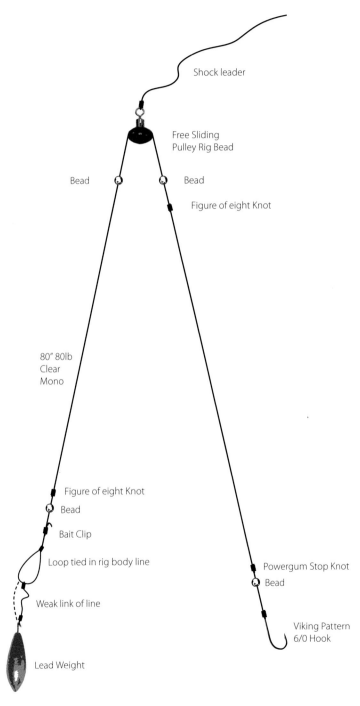

Shock leader

Free Sliding
Pulley Rig Bead

Bead   Bead

Figure of eight Knot

80" 80lb
Clear
Mono

Figure of eight Knot

Bead

Bait Clip

Loop tied in rig body line

Weak link of line

Powergum Stop Knot

Bead

Viking Pattern
6/0 Hook

Lead Weight

ONE UP/ONE DOWN RIG

This is my favourite rig when fishing deeper water, such as when fishing off piers and breakwaters straight down the side, or when casting close in. It also works well in deeper estuary channels when the angle of the line is steep in to the water as a general two-hook rig when fishing for plaice and flounder. Also for estuary codling and bass.

BUILD SEQUENCE

1. Begin with 40 inches of 60-pound clear monofilament line. At one end, tie on a size 4 swivel.
2. Slide on a five-millimetre bead, a size 4 swivel link to take the lead weight.
3. Slide on a rig crimp, 3-millimetre rig bead, size 6 swivel, another rig bead and a crimp. Leave these loose for now.
4. To the free end of the mono rig body, tie on a size 4 swivel.
5. Now slide the rig crimp assembly to within two inches of the top size 4 swivel, and crimp it in place.
6. The lower hook length is 20 inches of 20-pound Fluorocarbon, and the top hook length is 12 inches of 20-pound Fluorocarbon. The hooks are Aberdeen pattern size 2 when aiming for mainly smaller flatfish and whiting, or 1/0 when targeting medium sized fish such as bigger plaice and dogfish, but can be 3/0 when targeting bass or codling.

The longer hook trace, positioned just behind the lead weight, fishes hard on the seabed, but is totally free to move with the tide flow, giving both scent and visual attraction, plus natural presentation.

Because the bottom hook is free to slide some way on the main rig body, this also gives direct bite detection to the rod tip when fishing vertical, and when fish are suspicious and shy feeding, or slow to take the bait fully in.

The top hook puts a bait a couple of feet up in the water to take bonus free swimming round fish such as coalfish and pollack.

This rig is also very effective when fishing for shore turbot, not only in deeper water, but also when fishing for them in the shallow surf tables on a surf beach, or when fishing the flanks of estuary mouths. It is also the perfect way to fish a crab or lugworm bait on the bottom, with a fluttering fish or squid strip on the top hook to appeal to multiple species.

RIGHT RIG RIGHT TIME

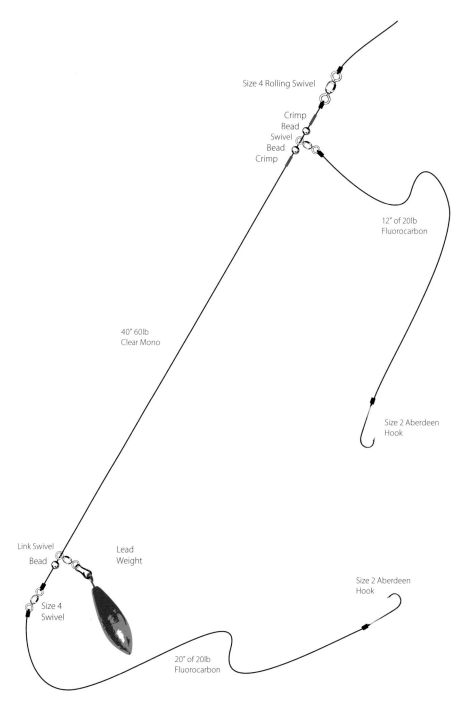

LONG AND LOW RIG

This rig features a very long hook trace that sits tight behind the lead weight, thus keeping the bait tight on the seabed, but free to wash around in any tide flow. This is a great rig for fishing in to deep water. It is ideal for fishing off deep water rock ledges on to sand when casting short to medium/long range, and off breakwaters and piers when you need to fish vertically straight below the rod tip for bigger fish such as rays, huss and even conger eels, big cod and bass.

BUILD SEQUENCE

1. Begin with 36 inches of 60-pound clear mono.
2. At one end tie on a bait/lead clip.
3. Slide on a rig crimp, three-millimetre bead, size 6 rolling swivel, another bead and a crimp. Leave these loose for now.
4. At the free end tie on an inverted bait/lead clip.
5. The hook trace is about 60 inches of 40-pound Fluorocarbon. Tie this to the free end of the swivel.
6. To the remaining end of the hook trace, tie on a size 4/0 Viking pattern hook.
7. Place the hook in the lower bait clip. Put the hook length inside the top inverted bait clip. Now slide the crimp and swivel assembly down the rig body line until it comes just tight and crimp in place.

With both the hook and the hook trace positioned correctly in the clips, during the cast the hook trace will stay secure and remain streamlined to aid casting distance. When the lead weight hits the sea, both the bottom hook and the hook trace will fall free of the clips and see the trace flow out in the tide as the rig settles on the seabed.

Being positioned close behind the lead weight, and being a long flowing trace, the bait is now free to move on the seabed with the flow of the tide and any surf movement. This creates a very natural free roaming presentation. Equally the bait is fishing hard on the seabed, exactly where big predators like winter cod, summer rays and bass will search for the majority of their food.

The reason I prefer Fluorocarbon over mono for the hook trace is that it is slightly stiffer, therefore is less prone to tangling when in moving water, but also it is more resistant to abrasion from teeth and general wear and tear. In fact, you can use a lighter breaking strain, say 30-pound Fluorocarbon instead of 40-pound or even 50-pound mono, due to this advantage, if you want to increase the movement of a bait.

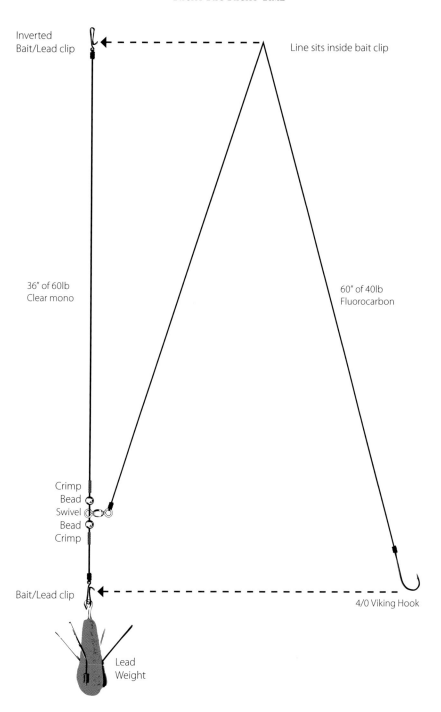

Inverted
Bait/Lead clip

Line sits inside bait clip

36" of 60lb
Clear mono

60" of 40lb
Fluorocarbon

Crimp
Bead
Swivel
Bead
Crimp

Bait/Lead clip

4/0 Viking Hook

Lead
Weight

This rig also encourages self-hooking by the fish. With the trace positioned tight behind the lead, and the trace flowing out in the tide, as a fish takes the bait, it invariably does so by approaching the bait from downtide as it follows up the scent trail. As it takes the bait, it will move forward a foot or two, before then turning back to swim with the tide. As it does so, it comes up hard against the grip-wired lead, which helps set the hook as the weight is pulled free.

Another advantage of this rig is that, when a fish is hooked, the lead weight is lifted upwards above the fish. This keeps it away from the worst of snags and helps reduce fish and tackle loss when fishing over mixed rough ground, or when fishing beyond rough ground on to clean sand, but having to retrieve back over the snags.

MULLET FLOAT RIG

I actually use two different types of float rig to cover different types of mullet fishing. The first is a simple bubble float set up that I can add water to, to add weight for longer range casting. I prefer the egg-shaped floats for this, not the round-shaped ones that look like UFOs.

BUILD SEQUENCE

1. Pass the main line through the eye of the jamming peg that fits inside the bubble float. Slide the line through the bubble float's central hole, pulling about 12 inches more through, then lock the line in place with the jamming peg.
2. To the end of the free tag end of line, tie on a size 8 swivel.
3. To the swivel, tie on five feet of six- to eight-pound Fluorocarbon, and add a size 6 to 12 short shank hook.

This casts well, and, with varying amounts of water added, can be cast a very long way to present bread and ragworm baits to distant mullet. I don't really watch the float for bites when using bubble floats. I watch the bread on the surface and for the mullet sipping down the bread. I find it more effective. It's a bit like watching a trout take a fly, count to two, then strike. However, you can wait until the float slides sideways as well and strike as it does so.

In situations where the mullet are only a few yards away and working deeper, I use a clear self-cocking waggler-type float.

1. On to your main line, slide a rubber float stop, then a size 10 swivel with a short two-inch length of fine diameter silicone tubing over the free eye. Slide on another rubber float stop.
2. Tie on a small size 10 swivel, or you can use a two-millimetre fly fisher's tippet ring if you think the mullet are extra spooky.
3. To the swivel, tie on two feet of four- to six-pound Fluorocarbon and a size 6 to 12 short shank hook.
4. The waggler is pushed in to the silicone tubing and can be easily removed and changed.
5. Cock the waggler to just show above the surface by adding split shot between the float and the tied swivel, and, to get the bait to drop quicker in the water, to the hook length mid-way between the hook and swivel.

The rubber float stops slide up and down on the line so are adjustable with regards to the height the float sits above the bait.

In very calm water, choose a shorter length waggler, but in a tide

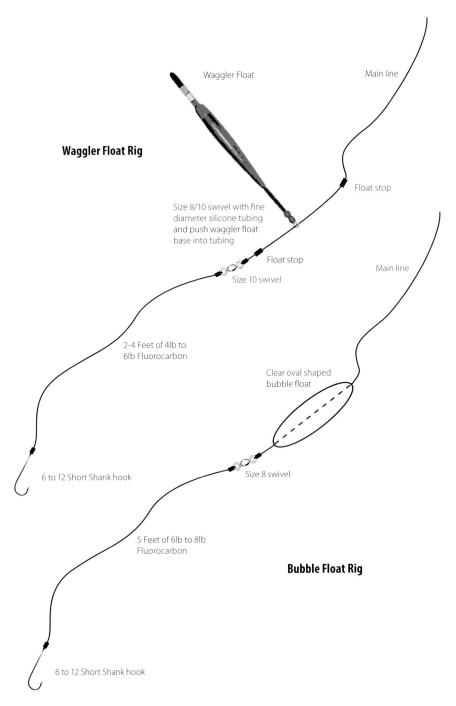

Waggler Float

Main line

Waggler Float Rig

Float stop

Size 8/10 swivel with fine
diameter silicone tubing
and push waggler float
base into tubing

Float stop

Size 10 swivel

Main line

2-4 Feet of 4lb to
6lb Fluorocarbon

Clear oval shaped
bubble float

6 to 12 Short Shank hook

Size 8 swivel

5 Feet of 6lb to 8lb
Fluorocarbon

Bubble Float Rig

6 to 12 Short Shank hook

current or a light chop, go for a longer bodied float to give it more stability.

When cocking the float, aim to get the top of the float above the surface by no more than two millimetres. This gives instant bite registration from the slightest interest. Again, black-topped floats, I feel, are the best.

For the hook length, I'd also suggest using the best and thinnest diameter Fluorocarbon you can afford. No, it's not cheap, but it doubles the number of bites you'll get, so is well worth it.

Something you rarely read about in mullet fishing, but it's also worth carrying some fly fisher's mud with you and run the full length of the Fluorocarbon through it so that it sinks under the surface quickly. Mullet have good eyes and will see line floating in the surface scum. They find it way less easy to see sunken Fluorocarbon.

GENERAL FLOAT RIG

A general float rig I use for wrasse, pollack, mackerel and garfish fishing is easy to build, and suits pretty much all float fishing situations, bar mullet. It can be used off piers, jetties, breakwaters, deep water rock ledges, and for working prawn baits over rough ground for bass and pollack, also whole sandeel.

The weight will lead the float out when casting, keeping things relatively tangle-free.

BUILD SEQUENCE

1. Onto your main line, slide a five-millimetre bead, and a cigar float.
2. Slide on a round ball-weight heavy enough to fully cock the float.
3. Slide on a five-millimetre bead, and tie on a size 6 swivel.
4. To the free swivel eye tie on 36 inches of 12- to 20-pound Fluorocarbon and add a size 2 hook for mackerel and garfish, or a 1 or 1/0 for whole sandeel.
5. Above the top bead, using a five-turn Grinner knot, tie on sliding stop knot from 14-pound Powergum, leaving the tag ends slightly long.

When choosing floats, the cigar-shaped ones are the best. They are stable, riding the sea swell easily, but also offer minimum buoyancy when a fish takes the bait. When weighting the float, try to balance it so that you can see no more than one inch or so of the tip of the float. This helps bite detection and again gives less pressure for a taking fish to overcome.

Float colours tend to be bright yellow and orange, but the fact is that black is the easier colour to see when viewed against water once the float is a few yards away and riding a swell. I paint my float tops black for this purpose, or invert them if they have a black base.

The sliding stop knot is the depth adjuster. Simply slide the knot up or down, using finger pressure, on the main line to adjust the depth the bait will fish below the float.

In the mentioned rigs you have enough to cover the majority of your fishing needs. As you gain more experience, you will modify them to suit the specific marks you fish, the ground feature and tides you come face-to-face with, and the fish you want to target. You'll also see other rig designs that might suit your fishing too. It's an ongoing process that will never end. These rigs have served me well, and they are a good platform to work on from.

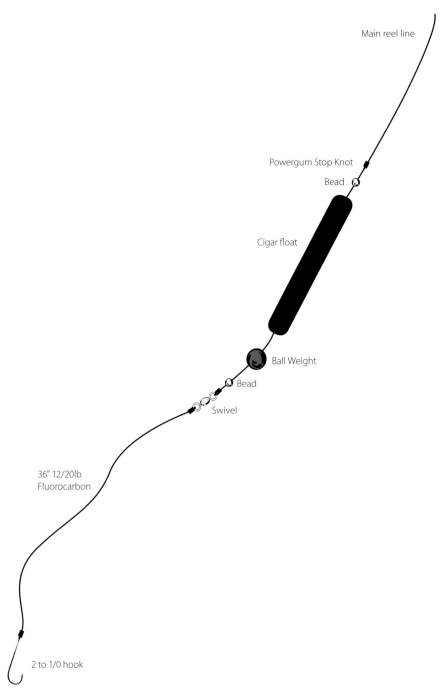

Main reel line

Powergum Stop Knot

Bead

Cigar float

Ball Weight

Bead

Swivel

36" 12/20lb
Fluorocarbon

2 to 1/0 hook

Chapter 11: Hooks

A dilemma faced by anglers fairly new to the sport is: what type of hook pattern is best for specific species, and how do you select the correct hook sizes to suit the type of fish you want to catch, and for the appropriate size of bait? Getting the right pattern and size of hook is crucial and one of the most important decisions we make when initially tackling up!

A good way to begin is to study the shape of the mouth of the species you expect to target. Compare, say, a flounder or plaice with a cod. The flounder has a small angled mouth designed to take small food items directly off the seabed, or to dig in to the sand and mud when the fish inverts and roots out shallow buried food. Cod, in comparison, and even smaller three-pound fish, have a big, open bucket shaped mouth designed to scoop up and suck in large food items, including live fish. A simple observation, but one that gives a clear indication that hook choice for these fish will be vastly different.

The flatfish, which gulps in food bit by bit from a static position, requires a narrow gape hook that they can easily take in to their mouths. The gape is the gap between the inner hook point and the inner shank of the hook opposite. Also, because flatfish tend to swallow hooks quite easily, a hook with a long shank will be easier to remove when releasing the fish. The common baits for flatfish are mainly worms, these being presented on the hook by being fed over the hook point and barb, slid round the gape, and then fed up the length of the hook shank to fully hide it. Again a long shank pattern is the best choice as it helps support and present the worm in a more natural posture. This type of hook is commonly called an 'Aberdeen' hook.

Some Aberdeen hooks for flatfish have a hook point at a slight outward angle when viewed against the straight shank. These are called 'Kirbed' and 'Reversed'. The Kirbed point leans to the left, and the Reversed leans to the right. This offset hook point is designed to get better contact in to the jaw of the fish as the fish backs or swims away and can be preferred by more experienced flatfish anglers. However, the greater the angle of the hook point in relation to the straight hook shank, the more direct pull power it takes to sink the barb.

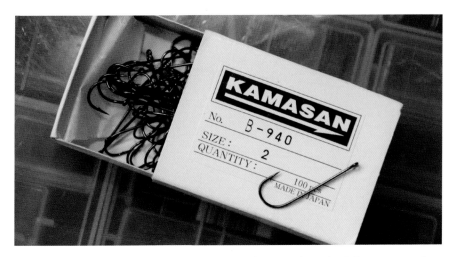

These smaller Aberdeen pattern hooks are also ideal for many other smaller species such as dabs, plaice, rockling, pouting, poor cod and whiting, immaterial of what bait you choose to use. Providing you keep the hook point well clear of the bait, the chances are the point will find a hold in the fish's mouth.

One important point, especially when working at ultra-long range, is to choose a pattern with a micro barb. Many hooks still have oversized barbs, which, when sunk in to the jaw of a fish, hold well and rarely fall out. The downside is that they need far more pressure applied to the hook point to fully sink the barb below the skin. When fishing at long range this may not happen and compromises the hook hold which can pull free and lose you a good fish. A small micro barb requires far less energy to fully pull the hook home, but holds almost as well as a bigger barb.

Moving on to fish with big open mouths and a feeding style that just hoovers food in, such as cod and bass, the narrow gape and long shank of the Aberdeen pattern hook becomes less effective as these fish need to be instantly struck as the bite occurs. For fish with big mouths we need to look at hooks with a shorter shank and an open gape between point and shank. These are commonly called 'Viking' pattern hooks.

The open gape between the inner hook point and opposite inner shorter shank means that the hook point has a greater chance of connecting with the inside of the mouth when the angler strikes. Equally important is that these fish can often be hooked in the scissors of the jaw, or close to the front of the jaw. This is because they are usually swimming forwards when they take the bait, so have momentum, then turn back to go with the tidal

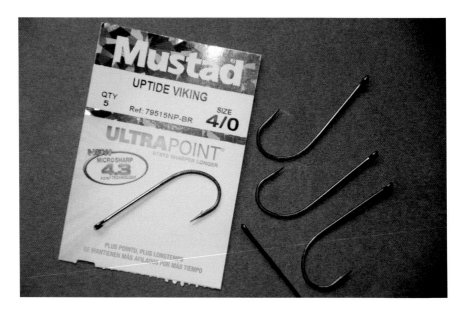

flow. If the hook is a long shank pattern and some of the shank is outside the mouth, as the line pulls on the hook it creates a leverage point where the shank touches the jaw, and this can see a light hook hold pull out as the pressure is then all on the hook point at an outward angle, not a direct pull pressure along the full length of the hook shank. The shorter shank hook reduces the chances of this leverage problem happening.

For this reason, I never use long shanked hooks for big round fish, such as cod and bass, or rays, preferring short to medium shank hooks that minimise this problem.

Some hooks are sold as 'wide gape' patterns. Again there are good and bad points to these. A wide gape hook means you can cram a large bait in to the gape, but still have the hook point well clear for contact with the fish. The disadvantage is that the further the hook point is away from the hook shank, the higher the leverage pressure on the hook point. Again this can increase the chance of the hook point being levered out, or springing out as the hook point flexes during the fight with a heavy fish if the line pull is at a sharp angle.

Shorter shank pattern hooks are also best for bulky baits such as crab, mussel, large fish baits and shellfish as the open gape gives more room to position the bait, but still keep the hook point well clear.

Furthermore, these hooks are ideal for big, slow feeders such as huss, rays and conger eels. These fish gulp in their food, but have big mouths, so a short to medium shank hook pattern is easier to take in, plus gets a good hold in the mouth when the fish is struck.

Some modern hooks have a high carbon content. Although these hooks are incredibly sharp and are great for smaller species, they can be prone to snapping when very heavy pressure is applied to them. This is why experienced anglers prefer a hook that has some spring in the temper of the metal allowing the hook to give slightly and attempt to pull straight under extreme heavy pressure. These are actually stronger than hooks that do not give at all. When targeting big fish, this is an important point.

For big conger eels, big rays, and other hard fighting fish, the hook characteristics stay the same as for the Viking hooks. However, these heavier hooks tend to be classified loosely as 'O'Shaughnessy' pattern hooks and have a much heavier gauge of wire and increased shank diameter for added strength.

When choosing hooks for bigger fish, including Viking patterns for bass, cod and rays, or O'Shaughnessy's for conger, I pick forged hooks for their strength. If you look at a forged hook, the sides of the hook gape and the lower to mid section of the shank will have flat sides. These have been flattened to improve lateral strength when pressure is applied to the hook point and eye of the hook by the line and pressure of the fish. Non-forged hooks can bend too easily with the gape of the hook opening and levering the hook point out.

I also always check new hooks in the packet before fishing with them. Even the best quality hooks can sometimes have rogue hooks in that have not been tempered or formed properly. Just try them in the fingers, or tie line to the eye, put the point in to a chunk of wood, and put the hook under a good pull pressure. This will confirm the hook has been tempered properly.

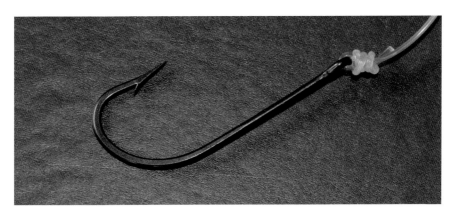

HOOK SIZES

To understand hook sizes, it is best to split the hook sizes in to two groups. One group with hooks quoted in figures without a 0 at the end, and the second group with hooks with a 0 after the number.

Hooks with no 0 are written as size 1, size 2, size 4, size 6 and so on. The size 1 hook is the biggest of this group, the size 2 the next smaller size, size 4 smaller still, and so on right down to a minute size 28, though hooks smaller than a size 12, other than for very small mini species, are rarely used in normal shore fishing.

Numbers with a 0 on the end are written as 1/0, 2/0, 3/0, 4/0, 6/0. The 1/0 is the smallest, the 2/0 a size bigger, 3/0 bigger still, and this scale goes right up to 12/0 for general use, which are shark hooks. The scale actually goes much higher, but these are not commonly used hooks in the UK. However, though manufacturers such as Mustad tend to adhere to the correct sizing of hooks, some other companies do not, so it is not a totally reliable sizing for all hooks.

There are many different makes and patterns of hooks and asking several experienced anglers which they prefer and what size they use will likely get you several different answers. However, established makes such as Mustad, Kamasan, Varivas and Sakuma have been around a long time and are arguably the most popular brands. These are the ones to judge all others by.

The list below is a basic guideline as to which hook pattern type and size is suitable for general species.

Fish	Hook Pattern	Hook Size
Sole Dab (small) Flounder (small)	Aberdeen Long Shank	Sizes 6 to 4
Flounder (large) Plaice Dab Whiting Coalfish (small) Pouting Rockling Dogfish Gurnard (small) Bream	Aberdeen Long Shank	Size 2 to 1

Plaice (large) Whiting (large) Shore coalfish Codling (small) Dogfish School bass Pollack Gurnard	Aberdeen Long Shank	Size 1/0
Bass Codling Cod	Viking	Size 2/0 to 6/0 depending on bait size used
Rays Huss	Viking	Size 3/0 to 6/0 depending on bait or lure size
Tope	Viking	Size 6/0
Shore ling	Viking	Size 3/0 to 6/0 depending on bait size used
Conger eels all sizes	O'Shaughnessy	Size 6/0 to 8/0 depending on bait size used and size of eels expected.

Also remember small strong hooks are just as capable of catching big fish as big hooks are if the angler plays the fish sensibly.

Use this table as a general guide. Only veer from it when you feel a specific bait size warrants a change in the size of the hook, such as when targeting specimen sized fish of a certain species.

SHARPENING HOOKS

Chemically sharpened hooks are ultra-sharp, or should be, straight out of the packet. These do not re sharpen well, and if you're a serious angler looking to maximise catches, my recommendation is that you use a hook once, then throw it away in to a safe and secure bin. Chemically sharpened hooks can also lose their sharpness quickly when dragged back through sand, mud, and especially clay, so make sure you constantly check your hook points when re baiting up.

The exceptions are the non-chemically sharpened Vikings and O'Shaughnessy's. These can be re sharpened using a small honing stone wetted with a little fine oil or saliva. In doing this, work the stone in upward vertical strokes towards the point, looking to thin the point just enough to get it to hook and hold in your finger nail when the point is dragged across it. The aim is to make the point fully sharp, but not over thin it and create a weakness that will see the point either turn and blunt if it comes in contact with a solid jaw, or break off on the strike. A fine honing stone is best as it cuts smoothly and can be worked slowly.

Always remember that the hook is the vital point of contact with the fish. Make absolutely sure you have the right pattern for the target fish, that it is the right size for the intended bait, and that it is ultra-sharp.

Chapter 12: Bait: Choice & Presentation

All too often, anglers spend hard-earned money on the best rods, reels and tackle, then skimp and penny-pinch when it comes to bait. Getting the best tackle you can afford certainly helps you fish more efficiently. Yet, without quality bait, no matter how good your gear is, or your skill level, your catches will be average at best, and more likely way below the level they should be.

The best way to guarantee good bait is to dig or collect yourself, and learn how to look after it to keep it fresh and lively. The other option, which is chosen by the vast majority of anglers nowadays, is to buy from quality suppliers, such as good tackle shops, or directly from reliable bait suppliers and diggers. This chapter, then, is not about digging bait, which is a physical and obvious task or chore, not a true tactic. Our interest is in choosing the right bait at the right time, looking after it, and then presenting it to the fish in the right manner.

FRIDGES AND FREEZERS

Buying bait from the shop for immediate trips is fine. What I often find, though, is that I have bait left over, and from what I've seen, other anglers do too, and in fair quantities. If you can fish again within a couple of days, that fresh bait will last for that short time period if you look after it. If you can't, then, unless you can freeze it, it will be wasted.

The best investment an angler can buy is a bait fridge. Storage space can be a problem, but if you can find room in a garage or shed, a small outlay can reap big rewards in money saved on bait, over time, that would otherwise be thrown away. Looking through shop windows for sale adverts, or trolling through local newspapers 'second-hand for sale' columns should soon turn up a good working model at an affordable price. If money is not so much of an issue, a new fridge gives a guarantee and peace of mind for a while if you're storing a fair bit of bait.

Ideally, you need a decent-sized fridge with four or five shelves inside. This is important as you need the room for multiple trays or containers.

Forget fridges with a freezer compartment, which are ok for short term storage of frozen bait, like a pack or two of mackerel, squid or sandeel, for a week or two, but they have neither the capacity nor the ability to keep frozen bait in good condition much longer than that short time period.

The next step is a full-on freezer working alongside the fridge. This again can produce a major saving once the initial purchase expense is out of the way. My advice, from experience, is to get the biggest one you can for the storage space you have. What seems big enough at the outset will soon be full and you'll be wishing you had gone for a larger freezer. Owning a specific bait freezer means you can buy frozen bait in bulk at cheaper prices in the quantities you need, plus you always have bait when you want to fish, even for spontaneous trips.

Get a freezer with several baskets, which allow you to separate baits in to types and have enough ready and to hand for immediate trips. I have enough in the baskets for a couple of trips, no more. This makes it easier to choose from the top and saves time rummaging through the main freezer. The bulk bait is in the main compartment. I use heavy-duty, clear plastic bags to separate the different baits, again to make things more obvious and accessible. If you mix and bury baits, it's a nightmare having to constantly take the whole contents of the freezer out to find a specific bait at the base of the unit.

What's essential is to always date bait. I like to use up bait within a maximum of six months, if possible. Modern freezers can keep bait much longer than that, but I like to keep a fresh turnover and minimise the chances of baits going stale.

Leftover fresh bait I want to freeze goes into the fast freeze compartment, which is always left empty for this purpose. Even when bait is fresh and packeted, if you have two or three flat metal trays inside the freezer and lay bait directly on to these, they freeze quicker. Reducing the freeze time minimises the chance of flesh softening and the first stages of decay setting in.

For carrying bait when going fishing, I use a large 30-litre cool box with ice packs in, capable of holding enough frozen bait for longer trips over a day or so with two of us fishing. A good quality, well-insulated box will keep bait frozen close to 24 hours if looked after, with the lid kept closed, and placed in a cool spot. Even longer in cooler weather.

For single, short duration trips, I have a smaller cool box that takes a freezer pack, two packs of mackerel, a couple of packs of sandeel, two wraps of black lug, and a box of squid, with a little room to spare. Perfect for a few hours' fishing. Keeping bait frozen until needed means, if it is still fully frozen, it can be put back in the freezer without waste. Any fresh worm I carry in paper or material in a small separate plastic container with a lid on in my tackle box, as I want them lively, not comatose through being too cold.

BAIT PRESERVATION, SEASON & PRESENTATION

BLOW LUG

Lugworm are the commonest bait used in the UK. There are, to keep it simple, blow lug, yellowtail lug and black lug. Blow lug are the smaller brown or red coloured lug found on salt flats in U-shaped burrows. Dense beds of them can be seen by their tell-tale circular casts on the surface of the sand.

These are a great fresh bait, but are hard to keep alive for long periods. Placed *en masse* in a bucket, the damaged ones quickly bleed in to the water which accelerates the dying process of the healthy ones. The best way to keep these for a short period of a few hours is to place no more than

12 worms in to clean, dry newspaper and anticipate using them as fast as possible. For longer storage, use cat litter trays with a couple of sheets of dampened newspaper in the bottom. Place the worms on to the newspaper well-spaced apart, then cover with another couple of sheets of newspaper and continue adding worms. If you constantly change the newspaper, and pick out any dead worms, you can prolong the process for two or three days, but beyond that is chance. Store them in a fridge that is cold, but not overly so. A typical temperature setting would be 3 degrees Celcius. They should not be not frozen when gutted, as when thawed they become soft and unusable.

Some anglers use cat litter trays with fresh sea water in to a depth of no more than three inches and place the live lug in these. There are claims of holding live worms for a week or more doing this. However, having clean sea water available for constant changing, and the time to be checking the contents daily, has never been an option for me, so I discount it.

I tend to treat yellowtail lug exactly the same, though they are tougher than blow lug. Like blow lug, I find any form of holding them beyond a couple of days sees their effectiveness deteriorate regards catching fish. I prefer fresh.

Blow lug are a good bait all year round. Being full of natural blood and scent they give a strong scent trail for fish to follow up and will take most

species of fish including all the flatfish, codling, bass, coalfish, whiting, dogfish, and even rays. They are especially good in coloured water after a rough sea, or at night when scent plays a greater part in attracting fish.

There are several schools of thought regards actual presentation, but I prefer to nip the bulk of the sandy tail off, but leaving just a little in place to avoid the worm bursting, then slide the worm on to the hook, tail first, trying not to burst the worms body, but bringing the hook out through the head end. This is where the bulk of the juice and blood is and the obvious place to position the hook point. Others put the head on the hook first, leaving the thinner tail at the hook point.

For single worms aimed at smaller fish, like flounder, dabs and sole, choose a long shank Aberdeen hook, its size roughly matched in overall length to the length of the worm. For bigger baits, slide two or more blow lug on to the shank of the hook, pushing them up on to the hook length, not worrying if you burst them. Now bind them with a little thin bait elastic to hold them in place for casting. This 'broken' presentation is a good one to choose when targeting fish in coloured water and at night, as it gives maximum scent.

One or two blow lug are also good as a tipping off bait positioned on the hook point below a bigger bait of black lug. This adds natural blood to the scent of the gutted black lug to increase its effectiveness.

BLACK LUG

Black lug are much bigger worms found on semi-lee shores and at the mean low tide mark in the more sheltered corners of surf beaches. They burrow much deeper than blow lug in burrows that are angled or near vertical. They will keep for a few hours in fresh seawater, but soon swell and again release blood that kills any healthy ones. The best way to preserve lug for the longer term is to nip the heads off and squeeze out all the guts as soon as you dig them. When you get home, dry the worms on absorbent kitchen paper, then wrap them, without the worms touching each other, in cling film, and freeze them straight away for long term storage. If they are to be used within a few days, just place them in the fridge in the cling film and they will hold well enough.

If you buy fresh but gutted black lug from shops, they are usually rolled in newspaper. This is okay for instant use. If you have any left after a fishing trip, then remove the unused worms from the newspaper, re-pack in cling film, and put them in the freezer. If left in newspaper, even in the freezer, air will access the worms through the paper and dry them out. Freezer burn through air contact is the kiss of death for all baits.

Incidentally, if you directly expose gutted fresh black lug laid on newspaper to damp air, say in a garage for a couple of days, it goes sticky to the touch. This is especially good for winter dabs, also cod. Another way to achieve this sticky touch with lots of smell is to freeze, thaw and refreeze black lug a few times.

Black lug is, arguably, another all-year bait, but it is far more effective during the autumn and winter months when these deeply buried worms are more likely to be washed out of their burrows. Live worms freshly dug have a lot of natural blood and juice, so are brilliant for coloured water and night time use. Once gutted they remain a good bait, but will lack the real pulling power of the ungutted lug. However, gutted black lug, and frozen black, will catch well in its own right, but benefits from tipping with the blow lug, a strip of squid, or shellfish such as mussel, razorfish or cockle, to add fresh scent.

Freshly dug black lug can be used whole, or in pairs, depending on size, presented on a two-hook Pennel hook system (one hook directly above another hook on the same hook length) and bound lightly with bait elastic for casting strength. Gutted black lug are presented the same, but pushed up the lower hook, and onto the hook length a short distance, then the moveable top hook slid down the hook length and positioned in the top of the bait. This gives a big fish, like a cod or bass, more chance of taking at least one hook in to its mouth immaterial of which end it attacks the bait. The top hook holds the bait firmly, but again a few turns of bait elastic will hold everything in place, and will stop smaller fish ripping the bait to pieces too quickly.

Another good trick is to place a whole razorfish up the length of the worm, or two or three mussels, then bind this together around the worm to form a rough sausage shape. These combination baits are very effective during, and immediately after, stormy seas when broken shellfish and worm are naturally washing ashore, but also when general fishing.

Black lug again targets a wide range of fish and can take pretty much anything on its day, but is especially effective for cod and bass.

KING RAGWORM

Capable of growing in excess of two feet in length, this predatory ragworm lives in mud and shingle inside estuaries, harbour flats, and in muddy mussel beds. It is, in my opinion, a good but not great bait for all manner of sea fish including cod, bass and flounders, but is especially effective in small chunks or pieces for mini-species, such as gobies, small wrasse, shannies and tompot blennies. King rag can also be localised with regards to its overall effectiveness.

Ragworm straight from the tackle shop usually comes wrapped in newspaper, but may be placed in dry peat, or sometimes vermiculite, which keeps the worms dry and lively. Keep them cool and they will last a good day or more without problem. For longer storage in the fridge, I place just a few rag in to a plastic container with a hole pierced in the lid to let air in as the worms must be able to breathe, in fresh peat, and again check every

day for dead and dying ones. Doing this will keep them lively and fresh for a few days. They do not freeze well at all, coming out as soft and mushy.

You can use small sections of broken-off king rag on smaller long shank Aberdeen hooks for flatfish and smaller species. For bigger fish, such as cod and bass, use the whole or a large section of a big worm, but I find it best as a combination bait with either blow lug, or with sandeel as a tippet bait over the hook point, or using king rag as a tippet below a big lug bait. Also try tipping a king rag with a small strip of squid or mackerel for rays and dogfish, or add a fillet of sandeel along the length of the rag to target small-eyed ray and dogfish.

Smaller whole king rag, or sections of large rag, can be effective under float tackle for pollack and wrasse when fishing off rock ledges in to deeper water. You hook the rag by passing the hook through the thicker end or head of the bait, leaving the tail section to wriggle.

I do not rate king rag as a great bait, personally. With this in mind I prefer to use them very quickly for something specific, such as mini species. They are readily available from tackle shops, so I choose to waste no time keeping them, but buy as I need them.

MADDIE RAG

These are the little red and orangey-red slim ragworm no more than three inches long that are found in rich estuary mud inside estuary creeks and mudflats, also in soft mud inside harbours. They are a brilliant bait for golden-grey and thin-lipped mullet, also flounder, school bass, as well as many general shore species.

For instant use, I just place them in newspaper inside a plastic tub and they are fine for the day. For longer periods, two to three days, I do much the same, but freshen the paper every day and check for any dead ones. The knack is not to have too many worms in the one container, and just keep them slightly damp with a light drizzle spray of fresh seawater kept in the same fridge to be at the exact same temperature. The paper seems to make them firm up a bit, without losing any of their liveliness. Forget freezing them, they just come out mushy and useless.

These are normally presented on short shank hooks, nicking the hook point through the very end of the head using several worms to form a bunch with the tails left free to wriggle. Alternatively, under light float tackle, slide one worm on to a fine wire short shank hook, leaving the tail wriggling free, and trot this down with the tide. They are also good in twos and threes nicked through the head and fished in front of a small spinning spoon for golden-grey and thin-lipped mullet.

They are also a good bait for daylight flounder, small mullet, smelt, and mini species fished on light Fluorocarbon hook lengths.

WHITE RAGWORM

These are the jewel in the angling bait crown. Revered by top freelance and match anglers as the best bait of all, especially when used during periods of low fish activity. What it is about the white rag no one seems to fully know, but it's likely rare for fish to come across them, as they can be very localised, and their scent may have something special in the form of body chemicals that improves their appeal to fish in relation to other baits. Also their body colour, being white, makes them more visible, and they are an active ever-moving worm. They are effective fished on their own, but can really hit form when used as a tippet bait below other worm baits.

They are very localised, preferring shale and seed mussel beds, but will also be found adjacent to rocks and rock ledges and reef ground that butts on to sand, and often in areas of clean sand where tube worm colonies exist at the heads of small estuaries and on surf beaches. Small white rag will also be found in muddy estuaries along the edge of mud flat creeks.

The best marks tend to be on ground that only uncovers a few times each year on the very biggest spring tides. Timing the tides to coincide with offshore winds and high pressure will see the tides push further out than predicted and see you working what is technically virgin undug ground with much improved yields. Expect the worms to be deep while the tide is ebbing, but come nearer the surface when the tide turns and starts to flood. Often the big low tides will fall in darkness, so be prepared to dig at night using a powerful headlamp.

White rag keeps best in a dark environment, so it's best to remove the automatic light bulb from the fridge that comes on when the fridge door is opened as they do not like too much natural or artificial light, even in brief doses.

Whites are best placed in cat litter trays, or similar, that can stack neatly on top of each other. This makes the maximum use of the available space. In to the trays add either coarse sand, or, better still, coral sand (available from aquarium shops) to an even depth of about 20 millimetres. Make sure this is washed through and fully clean. Add fresh sea water to a depth 12 millimetres above the sand, then put this in the fridge to cool for six hours. Now add no more than 25 white rag to a tray. The rag will then have enough room to remain separated when burrowing in to the sand and it limits the chance of them biting each other.

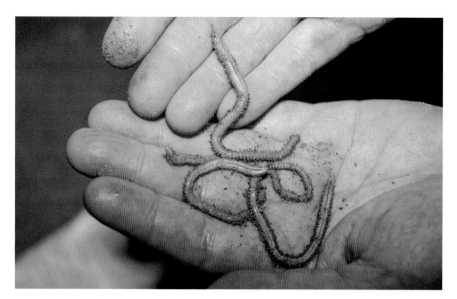

I change the coral sand for new every month or so. You can clean and re-use it, but I prefer not to. I change to fresh seawater every week, using seawater already chilled in the same fridge to the same temperature. Regards temperature, two to three degrees Celsius is about right. Try to minimize repeated opening of the fridge door leading to fluctuating temperatures inside. Whites stay fresh best if the overall temperature remains constant. The most important point with white rag is to keep the trays fully clean, try not to over-handle them, check for any dead or wounded worms and remove them immediately. It is possible to keep white ragworm for months, but they are a rare commodity for me, so they tend to get used pretty quickly. White rag, again, do not freeze well and are better used fresh.

These are an incredible bait fished as whole small worms, or in sections of bigger broken-off worm on long shank Aberdeen hooks. Keep the hook size small and slide the worm fully over the hook on to the hook length for perfect presentation. When used as a tippet bait, slide a small section over the hook point below a lug or shellfish as it tends to encourage a taking fish to attack the hook point first.

White rag takes a wide variety of species and will often take fish out of season that you don't even realise are there. This is the best bait to have when bites and fish are few and far between, especially in the difficult period between late January and mid April when inshore fish stocks are at their lowest ebb. It gives you a real edge, though, any month of the year!

SHORE CRAB

One of the most important and effective baits the sea angler has. Crab are found hiding in amongst rocks, boulders, under weed from low to high tide line, in mud, at the edge of sand where it meets rocks and weed, and in man-made structures under bridges, piers, jetties, and even in man-placed traps such as drainpipes, old tyres, in fact anywhere they can find some shelter and protective cover.

The reason they need cover is that, in order to grow, they need to shed their old shells and grow new ones. To do this, they extract calcium from the old shell, making it brittle, while at the same time forming a new soft shell underneath. This is called a peeler crab and is a top bait full of natural scent. They then swell the soft new body by taking in water which forces off the back of the old brittle shell, and force themselves free of the now redundant shell. Now with no protective outer shell, they hide under any available cover while taking in nutrients from the seawater that slowly harden the soft shell to form the new hard outer shell. This takes a few days, depending on the temperature of the sea and air. While the new shell is soft they are at their most vulnerable, hence the need to find cover.

Crab can be found as individuals, but also you'll find a male crab carrying a smaller female around. The one underneath, if it's facing downwards, will be a peeler or very close to popping its shell. The male crab carries the female with him until she is ready to mate. If the underneath crab is positioned belly to belly, then they are mating and the underneath crab will be a softie.

A quick way to sort peeler crab in the field while collecting is to feel the back of the shell. If it feels soapy to the touch, then it's a peeler. Alternatively nip off the end segment of one of the back legs. If it reveals a new perfectly formed soft leg end, then it's a peeler. If removing the end segment leaves only white sinew, then the crab is a hardback and should be returned. Incidentally, removing the segment of leg does the crab no permanent harm as this regenerates when the crab next peels.

In the southwestern corner of the UK, namely Devon and Cornwall, peeler crab can be found pretty much all year round due to the generally milder climate. However, the further north you are, the later the crab begin to peel due to slowly building temperatures. In South Wales the crabs start peeling around early March, but in North Wales it's mid to late March. In Cumbria mid April, and correspondingly so along the east coast. This is not exact and depends on the weather patterns at the time. In the north of Scotland the season may not start until late May and

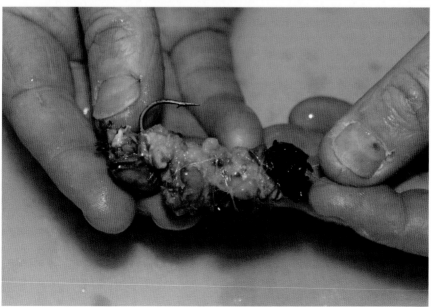

will end in September. Further south, mid to late October is classed as the end of the season for peeler crab, but again depends on the weather patterns prevalent at the time. It's no coincidence that the beginning of the crab peel coincides with the return of the majority of fish after late winter spawning. The peeling crabs give these thin and out-of-condition fish a major inshore nutritious, high-calorie food supply that quickly starts to restore their fitness.

Crab will peel throughout the quoted season, but there will be a gradual increase in numbers with the second set of spring tides in April, and then again during the spring tides in May and June seeing an explosion of peeling crab. Their numbers reduce noticeably through July and August, but by the second big tides in August and the early spring tides in September, again expect an explosion, especially if the tides coincide with previously hot and settled weather. Persistent flood water flowing in to estuaries has an adverse effect on peeling crab numbers, so also bear this in mind.

It has to be said that there are means by which you can keep large numbers of crabs in tanks, and by raising the temperature of the water induce them to peel. This book is about fishing tactics, though, not spending major amounts of time in the care of live bait. I choose to collect my own crab, which can be kept easily for well over two weeks with care, or can be bought at tackle shops and from bait dealers live and ready to fish with. The money, time and space required to keep crab in number in special tanks is above and beyond what the vast majority of anglers have available, or are willing to spend. We have to be realistic with the time we have!

For general storage, I pick through the crab immediately I get home, separating the not quite yet ready to peel, almost peeling, and soft crab. To identify the different stages of the crab I press on the back shell of the crab between the hind legs. If it is hard and unyielding, the crab is not near peeling. If the crab's back shell cracks under pressure and you see a definite crack around the edge of the shell where the back shell is leaving the body shell, then the crab is about to peel and is the perfect bait. The soft crab already peeled and without their discarded shell I place again separately. If you put peeler crab and soft crab in the same pot, the peelers can cuddle the soft crab and crush them.

Ready to peel crab and softies are my immediate baits, and these I carry in a small cool box with an ice pack and wet weed added. This keeps the crab for a few hours while I'm fishing and allows me to return any unused ones back to the fridge.

Live storage of crab, say for a week to two weeks, is easy. I use plastic ice cream containers with a sealable lid. Make a couple of small holes in the corners of the lid to allow air in for the crabs to breath. Only put around eight to ten crab in one plastic container, and add fresh, damp seaweed such as bladderwrack. Keep the container and weed damp by wetting it with fresh seawater every day. I change the weed every three days to avoid it going slimy. I also make sure the crabs get a drink of fresh seawater by putting a shallow depth of water in to a cat litter tray and letting the crabs drink for a few minutes, then replace them in their original container. Do not leave them in water. It is important to keep them hydrated, but do not allow them to take on enough water to start swelling their body and peeling. You can store soft crab exactly the same. Keep them clean, lightly hydrated, and they'll keep fine.

If you want to accelerate the peeling process, you can help induce this by introducing the crab in to water of a higher temperature than that found in the fridge. Do this gradually and let them drink enough to allow the swelling of the body process to begin. If you look, you'll see the crab blowing bubbles from the mouth, indicating they are taking on water. This can work in reverse, too, introducing a close to peeling crab to colder conditions to slow the process down by placing them in the fridge.

Peeler crab can be frozen very successfully, but it takes a little care. For freezing, I kill the crab by pinching it firmly between the eyes to crush the shell. Pull the legs away from the body to leave just whole body. Now peel off all the shell, top and bottom, to leave just a soft body. Remove the fawn coloured gills, sometimes called 'dead man's fingers', by pulling them fully out. These can carry bacteria that will accelerate the decomposition of the crab meat. Now lightly rinse the body under a cold water tap to remove any bacteria. Finally, fully wrap the crab body in cling film, making sure there is no access for air to enter, and place the crab packages on to a metal tray that has been in the freezer for a few hours. The metal tray helps the crab to freeze down a little quicker. Done like this, the crab will keep for months in the freezer, and I regularly freeze down summer crab for winter use, and late autumn crab for early spring use, retaining the majority of its effectiveness.

You can also freeze the crab legs and claws in the same way, peeling the legs off the shell and placing them in cling film. These are good to add as tippets to crab and other baits to hide the hook point, as the claws are good baits in their own right.

For big fish, such as bass and cod, the bait does not need to be neat on the hook. In fact, it needs to be a little mashed up to release as much scent as possible. With fresh whole peeler crab I remove the legs and take all the shell off the body leaving just the soft meat. If the crab is large, say twice as big as a 50p coin, I cut the crab body in half and feed one half on to the hook and bind it in to a sausage shape with bait elastic. If the crab is the size of a 50p coin or less, then I use both halves to again form a big bait. This is ideal for all night fishing situations as it oozes out a large amount of scent, but also for targeting bigger bass and cod when fishing at close to medium range in to rough, rocky ground. This smashed-up presentation also works well for rays, plaice and big flounder. Baits bigger than a golf ball will see fish grab and run with them, but struggle to swallow them in far enough for the hook to get hold.

Also try tipping a section of crab with a small sliver of mackerel, which is a great bait for rays. Crab is also a good tippet bait in its own right when placed below lugworm, ragworm and squid for fish such as rays, cod and bass, also huss, dogfish, conger and bream.

A neat trick when fish are shy biting and reluctant to take the full bait in to their mouths, or when they seem to play with the bait picking it up and dropping it repeatedly, is to take the shell off the body and cut it in half, but leaving the legs attached each side. Position the legs up the shank of the hook and bind the legs to the hook shank, and the soft body in to the bend of the hook, leaving the hook point well clear. This forces the fish to take the bait at the hook point, ensuring improved hook ups. This also works well when fishing in shallow, clear seas for bass that can be hook-shy.

When using smaller baits on smaller hooks, such as short shank hook types when targeting smaller flatfish, use a small section of body to cover the hook shank and bend, then slide on two or three peeled crab legs. This gives a very natural presentation when fishing in clear water and disguises the hook point from the fish.

MACKEREL

Bought frozen mackerel is a good stand-by to have in the freezer. It works throughout the year for a huge number of fish and is exceptionally good for predators, including huss, conger, rays, tope, also winter flounder, dabs, dogfish, and whiting.

When buying from a shop, always take a cool box with ice packs added with you, and, on purchase, place the frozen mackerel in to the box immediately. If fishing straight away, only buy enough for immediate

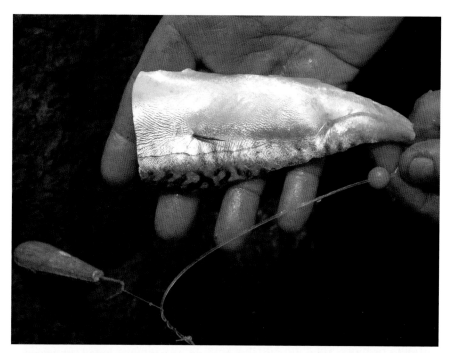

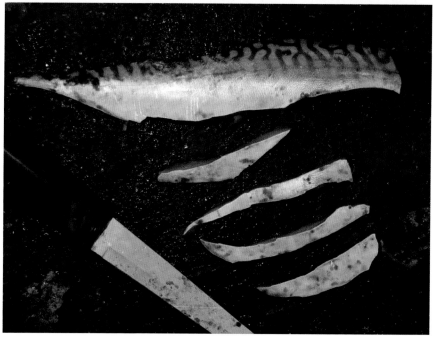

use. If buying for future trips, the cool box is equally important and keeps the mackerel in good shape until you get home. When selecting packs of mackerel in shop freezers, try to do this yourself, not relying on one of the staff. If the packs have a lot of frozen blood squashed in to the corners, the mackerel has been part thawed at some stage and will be soft-fleshed. Also look at the eye of the mackerel. If the eye is bloody and the flesh a dull green and greyish on the sides, the fish has again been either partly thawed, or was not fully fresh when frozen. Fresh mackerel that was blast-frozen quickly should have little if any blood in the packet, the eye and flanks should be clean, and the body colours still partly iridescent.

If you buy in bulk from a bait supplier who ships by courier, make sure someone is in for the delivery and immediately get the frozen bait in to the freezer. Do not let bait sit for even 30 minutes as it will begin to thaw out. Even when sent in polystyrene trays, the fish on the outer sides of the parcel may start to soften over roughly 24 hours of delivery travel time. Pick these out and use them as quick as you can.

If you catch fresh mackerel for bait yourself, then again the cool box and ice packs, or, better still, loose ice, will preserve them best. If you're close to home, leave the guts in. If you have some travel time of a couple of hours or more, then gut the mackerel before placing them on ice. This will keep the flesh fully firm. The guts are the last to chill and bacteria will set to work immediately, quickly ruining the flesh. Leaving the guts in, though, adds more scent when you're fishing for predators like tope and huss. When you get home, place single mackerel in to cling film and place them in the freezer. Single mackerel are better than putting them in twos or threes as they allow you to select just enough for what you want, plus freezes the individual mackerel quicker.

For big fish, tope, rays and huss, big bass and conger eels, neatly cut presentation is not overly important. You can fish small mackerel up to eight inches in length whole, just cutting the tail off to stop it spinning, or cutting the fish in half. I prefer the latter as it gets more scent in to the tide. I like to slash one side of a whole small fish to release more scent. The way to mount the hook in these baits is to pass the hook point in to a cut end, then pass it back and forth through the flesh and coming out of the skin two or three times, much like stitching, until the hook point comes out either two-thirds of the way down the length of the bait, or out near the front of the gill cover for a head section. This puts the hook point well clear of the bait for good hooking. Lastly, secure the bait to the hook with plenty of bait elastic for security when casting. The bait elastic also helps the bait stay intact on the seabed longer and is less prone to quick stripping by crab and smaller fish *etc.*

Cut presentation becomes much more important when you target fish allowing the bait to drift through the surf tables using a light lead weight, or travel with the tide through deeper channels and down sand bank inclines. Fish like sizeable turbot, rays and tope being obvious targets. This requires a full fillet to be taken from one side of the mackerel. The mackerel needs to be thawed to do this neatly.

The easy way to do this is to make a cut across the width of the mackerel directly behind the pectoral fin. Hold the mackerel by the tail, cut in to the tail facing away from you, and slide the knife, which needs to be sharp, up towards the first cut behind the head until the whole fillet comes free. With the fillet on a cutting board, now cut the fillet either in half lengthways for a big bait, or in to thinner strips for more movement.

Any fillet or bigger strip used for casting will need securing with wraps of bait elastic wound around the fillet that is in contact with the hook shank. I prefer to pass the hook through the skin side of the fillet first, then back through the flesh side, pass the fillet over the eye of the hook so that the top of the fillet is on the hook length, then add turns of elastic thread above and below the hook's eye to secure it, but leaving the main fillet still free to move below the hook.

To cut fish strips for smaller species, I again take the fillet off, then cut the strips at an angle across the fillet's width. It also pays to cut off excess flesh to create more movement in the bait. The white belly section is perfect for this as it reflects light and looks more like a live fish as it moves in the tide. When cutting fine thin strips for smaller species, a good tool to carry is a craft knife, like a Stanley knife or modelling knife. These allow more precise cutting than a standard knife will. Always cut on a proper modern moulded cutting board. This gives a stable base for neatness, but also keeps the knife sharp.

As before, wrap the upper end of a smaller fish strip securely to the top of the hook, and around the shank too, for long range casting, but leaving some strip free to move below the hook.

HERRING

Herring can also be used frozen all year round, but is most effective used seasonally. Its prime time is early spring and late autumn when the herring shoals are usually working close inshore in many areas and hunting fish will then be naturally finding wounded, dying, and smashed-up herring on the seabed.

When buying fresh herring, look that the eyes are not sunken or very bloody, the gills inside are still red, and the body silver with a flush of green and still bright with some firmness. If the flesh feels soft, then the fish is old. Smell is also a good indicator as if the herring smells of anything other than the sea, then it is past its best.

It will take all manner of species, but is especially good for spring time rays, especially thornbacks, also tope, huss and conger. Fillet as for mackerel, but also use it whole, in halves, or in chunks just cut straight across the body. Herring in strip form, cut as you would with mackerel, is also a top bait for dabs, whiting, and dogfish.

BLUEY

This is a relatively new bait for sea fishing which was first used around 2008 and imported from Iceland and Norway where it was used for commercial long line bait targeting cod. It is a Pacific saury, looking a little like a garfish, but is much more oily even than mackerel. It is bought frozen, usually in packs of three or four, but also in larger boxes. Again check the eyes for heavy blood clotting, and for signs of past partial thawing with diffused colouring on the flanks and juice in the corners of the packets.

The elongated body is good in length sections suitably cut to target rays, tope, conger eels and huss, but also as strip baits for all manner of smaller fish, such as whiting, dogfish, and flatfish. It is also good for cod, in fact better than mackerel in my opinion when fishing deep water from the shore over rough ground, even though fish, as such, is not the first choice cod bait.

Stitching the hook in and out of the body length to bring the hook point out near the lower end, then applying a good wrap of bait elastic, secures everything neatly and tightly for casting. Due to the high oil content, this bait does not wash out as quickly as mackerel or herring will, so it can be left for longer when targeting fish such as big eels, rays and tope on ground that is not heavily populated with smaller bait fish that are constantly ripping at the bait.

There is no real season for bluey; use it every month of the year with confidence.

SANDEEL

Bought or caught fresh and kept alive in aerated seawater, sandeels will keep active for an hour or two, longer with better aeration, but keep them cool and try to change the water regularly while fishing, say every 20 minutes. They are excellent fished under float tackle for bass and pollack, but will also take many other species including mackerel, coalfish and wrasse. Hook them by passing the hook through both jaws, bringing the hook point out roughly half way between the eyes and the point of the nose.

Bought frozen in packs they are an essential bait to have in the freezer. When buying frozen, check the eyes for excessive blood, and if the flanks of the sandeel look dull white, then they have either been partially unthawed, or have suffered freezer burn and exposure to air. The flanks should be a constant natural colour.

They work most of the year through, and can be used to target rays, especially small-eyed ray and spotted ray, bass, dogfish, turbot, huss, pollack and cod, also in small sections or strips for whiting, dabs, flounder *etc.*

To present a whole frozen sandeel, I prefer to cut off the tail, pass a long shank Aberdeen hook, chosen to suit the size of the sandeel, through the cut end, passing it as far as it will go down the body, then bringing the hook out and putting the point back in to that same exit hole, stitching style, and repeat until the hook comes out around the gill cover of the sandeel. Pull the hook trace straight inside the eel, then bind everything

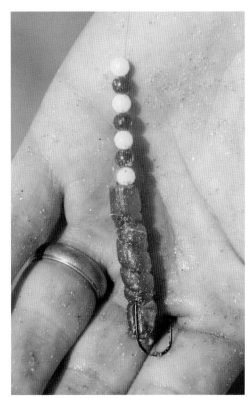 

with thin elastic thread. If you want a bigger bulkier bait, put one sandeel on the hook as before, then place a second sandeel, this time head to tail with the first, and bind with elastic. Smaller sections, I again choose the hook size to suit the bait by length, then pass the hook down through the length of the bait and secure with elastic thread.

Regards hook sizes, when choosing, the gape of the hook needs to be large enough to have the hook point well proud of the bait for easy contact with the fish.

Make sure you carry frozen sandeel to your fishing in a small cool box with packs of ice to keep the sandeel fully frozen. While fishing, only remove what you will immediately need. Sandeel softens quickly when unfrozen.

I have sandeel available for use right through the year as it is one of the most consistent baits. You will find, though, that, in many areas, it really comes in to its own from May onwards with the summer and autumn months seeing it at its very peak.

SQUID & CUTTLEFISH

There are several options with squid. The standard squid most frequently sold is Californian squid, often called calamari, which is bleach-washed to make it look white for the domestic market. This works fine and catches a lot of fish, but the washing process does see it lose some of its natural scent. There is also 'dirty' squid; this is often, but not always, *Loligo vulgaris*. This is unwashed natural squid. Some say it works better than standard squid. I use it, and find the dirty variety does work especially well with conger and bull huss. There are also small squid called *Loligo japonicus*; these are about one inch to two inches long, and work well either as individual baits or using several together to form a bigger sausage-shaped bait.

Squid can be bought fresh from food suppliers, but most squid for angling is bought frozen, either in packets of a few depending on size, in one-pound (by weight) boxes, or in five-pound boxes. For easy storage and carrying, packets, or better still the one-pound boxes, are best. Carry the packs and boxes in a cool box, and, as always, take out only what you immediately need. Squid will refreeze a couple of times and still catch well, but it's best freshly frozen and should look white. If it carries a pink tinge, then the decomposition stage has set in and the bait is past its best for the majority of species. Stale, stinky squid fished whole, though, has taken many a big autumn bass and lazy conger, so remember this if all else fails.

Buying five-pound boxes can save a fair bit of money. However, you need to partially thaw the squid, then repack them in to convenient zip-lock bags with, say, four to six squid in. The partial thawing will not spoil the squid.

Whole squid is good for bass and conger, but also cod, and if not too big, for rays too. I prefer to use a two-hook Pennel rig for whole squid with the top hook sliding free above the first. I pass the lower hook down through the whole length of the squid's body and bring it out through the head and between the tentacles. The top hook is passed in to the top end of the body, then I wrap the lot with bait elastic to form a long sausage shape. Do not leave the head below the hook. Fish have a habit of nipping off the free-swinging head and missing the lower hook.

Also, fish squid in long strips cut from the body, either as an individual bait, or alongside lugworm as a splint or as a tippet on the hook point below lug and rag baits. In half body, or big chunks, it works well for rays, huss and conger, and is a great combination bait with mackerel, herring and bluey for rays, conger and huss.

Smaller thin strips are good for tipping worm baits for whiting and

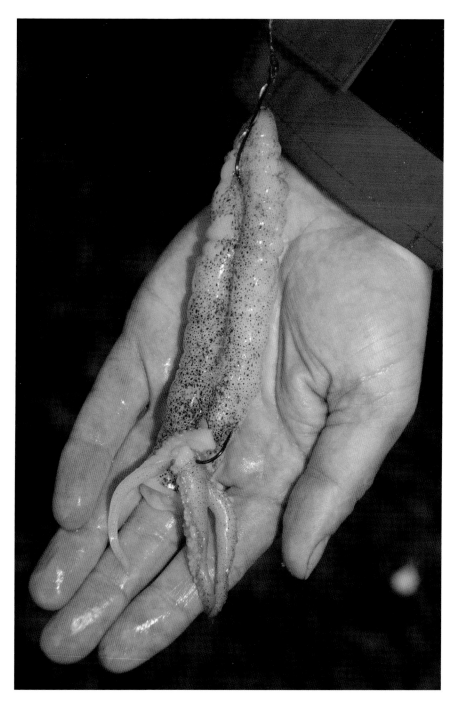

dabs, also dogfish. Thin strips of squid can also be used as splints to help secure softer baits, such as mussel and small blow lugworm, to provide lateral support so that, with an overlay of bait elastic, they can be cast to extreme ranges without fear of the bait breaking up to any major degree.

I also use a wide section of squid to act as a tough outer armour for softer baits, such as mackerel, that are coming under attack from small fish and crab and being stripped down overly quickly. It's simply a matter of folding the squid fully over the mackerel, or other soft bait, then binding with bait elastic to form a compact sausage shape. The squid also acts as a wrap that stops the tide flow from washing out a bait too quickly. Adding the squid over a scent-laden bait can prolong the seabed life of bait at least twofold. The scent trail from the bait may be weaker than normal, but it travels further as it disperses longer, and can pull in fish that would otherwise be missed.

Cuttlefish are prepared in the same way, but cuttlefish is thicker and tougher in consistency than squid, and is better cut as bigger baits for conger eels, which it is excellent for, but also for bass and cod.

Squid and cuttlefish can be fished 12 months of the year, but squid is especially effective in the late summer months and through the autumn in to winter.

PRAWN

Prawns bought from supermarkets, either fresh or frozen, will catch fish, but are only classed as a standby bait. The prawn you need are the rock pool prawns you catch yourself in little nets and keep alive in buckets of often-changed sea water. Try to keep them cool by placing the bucket in a rock pool and in the shade if possible for almost immediate fishing.

When freezing, put them whole as they are on to metal trays that are already positioned in the freezer, and, when frozen, put them in half dozens in a small sealable bag.

They are effective, especially alive and fresh, under floats for bass and pollack, but also take wrasse too. I nick the hook once through the end of the tail a little way in from the tail fin. This allows the prawn to move fairly naturally. If the fish nip off the body and miss the hook, slide the hook from the tail further down the length of the body bringing the hook point out nearer the head.

Prawn can also be used for ledger fishing fished on a hook length long enough to give the bait a little movement. Alternatively pull the rod back a few inches at a time and retrieve a little line to simulate the backwards

movement of the prawn, which is deadly for bass and also flounder. It will take bass and whiting just fished static, but also is very good ledgered for thornback rays. It is a little-used bait, generally speaking, as many people do not realise its true effectiveness. For long-range casting, choose a hook that will slide down the length of the body, bringing the hook point out through the head. A little bait elastic will hold it in place. Put another prawn alongside the first and then wrap in elastic for a bigger bait.

You would be tempted to think that prawn are mainly a summer bait, and for float fishing they are. However, they are good in winter, even at night, but should be regarded as an alternative, not main bait.

MUSSEL

Mussel are visually easy to find and can be seen clinging to exposed rocks on surf beaches, found in dense beds in the mouths of estuaries, attached to harbour walls, groynes, the support legs of jetties and piers, and can also be found on rocks and in amongst weed along the sides of estuary banks. You will also find mussels attached to boat mooring ropes and chains exposed at low tide.

They are virtually always accessible, immaterial of the size of the tide, though a tide well on the ebb and either side of low water is the best time to pick as the majority of mussels are exposed.

The bigger offshore mussels, sometimes called horse mussels, can also be found along the low water line occasionally, usually after a storm when they have been scoured out by rough seas and washed ashore.

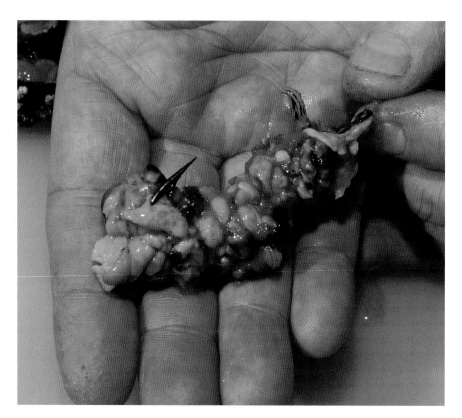

Mussels are usually in big numbers attached together and will cover a large area. However, do not just pick huge clumps of attached-together mussels; be selective and choose only the biggest. Never pick too many from the same area either, just one or two, then move a short distance away. This helps preserve overall stocks and does not weaken their communal structure. They use this communal grouped construction to help them stay attached to rocks in bad weather and rough sea swells, so it is important to remember.

Mussel will keep quite happily for up to a week in a bucket of seawater, providing you change it every day with fresh seawater. If you leave the water to stagnate, the mussels start to smell and will die. Remove any that start to open their shells. You can also keep mussel alive by laying them on, and covering them with, newspaper soaked in seawater. Kept cool like this in a bait fridge, again a week or so is possible, providing you remove any with an open shell as these are dying.

To remove the mussel from its shell, the best tool is an old blunt butter knife or short-bladed knife with the blade cut down to be no more than two inches long. Another good tool is an old teaspoon with the end smoothed down a little.

If right-handed, take the mussel in the left hand with the curved inner edge with the beard pointing towards you. Force the edge of the knife or spoon in to the crack between the two shells exactly where the beard is and twist the knife to semi open the shell. Run a knife inside the two shells up towards the point or head of the mussel, fully round the back and up to the beard. The top shell now comes away, leaving the mussel in the lower shell. Run the knife or spoon all the way around the bottom shell and the whole mussel will come free. This process is called skeening.

For bait you want to use immediately, that is all you need to do. However, mussel flesh is toughened and the smell factor increased if they are steeped or soaked in their own juice in the fridge for a couple of days. Use either a good watertight plastic container, or a jam jar with a lid. It is a simple case of just putting the skeened-out mussel straight in to the container and letting them sit in their own juice. This is ok for up to three or four days, but after that the juice starts to ferment, so aim to use the bait within that time.

To freeze skeened mussel, dry them on some kitchen towel then place them individually on a metal tray that has been in the freezer for a few hours and pop them back in the freezer. This helps the mussel freeze quicker. When frozen, put them in sealable plastic bags of about a dozen. Done like this, they will keep months.

There is a knack to securing mussel to the hook. Depending on the size of the mussels, slide two or more on to the hook and make sure a little of the flesh is up over the hook eye and the knot. Make multiple wraps of bait elastic up and down the mussel, aiming to form a tightly wrapped sausage shape. One mussel may be enough for flatfish, but for bigger fish like cod, use several mussels and make a sausage-shaped bait up to four inches long. Done properly like this, mussel can be cast a long way without fear of it breaking up.

Mussel also makes a good combination bait with lugworm. It is simply a matter of using the worm as a splint, laying the mussel up the length of the worm, then wrapping with bait elastic. Or add the mussel as a tippet bait at the hook point.

A good way to fish a big mussel bait is to take a whole squid, pull out the head to leave the empty body cavity, fill the cavity with mussel, then bind the cavity closed with bait elastic. Slide the squid parcel over the hook and up the shank on to the hook length, bringing the hook point out at the lower end, and wrap securely along the full length of the parcel with bait elastic. Puncture the squid a few times with the point of a knife to release the juices. This is a good dodge when crabs are picking away at soft baits, and when quickly destroying exposed mussel. The crabs cannot get through the squid flesh as quickly, keeping the bait intact and releasing scent for longer.

Mussel is especially good for flounder, dabs, plaice, coalfish, whiting, dogfish, codling and cod on both surf and rough ground beaches, bass again over sand and rough ground, sometimes thornback rays too. Very small bits of mussel, including the tongue, fished on very small size 10 hooks, will also catch difficult-to-tempt sole when they seem impossible to take on any other bait.

Mussel is a year-round bait, but results are always best just after winter storms when some mussel have been broken up along the shore as the fish can then become preoccupied with them. This is when they are deadly as a tippet bait too, below lugworm. Naturally they are also effective inside estuaries fished in close proximity to seed mussel beds and can be deadly for plaice in this scenario.

COCKLE

Cockle are common and seen on sandy/muddy estuary salt flats, often sitting just proud of the surface as you walk along. They can be used all year round.

They will catch used as a single bait taking flounder, small bass, black bream, eels, whiting, dabs and sometimes plaice. Just pass the hook through the centre of the cockle body and bring the hook point out through the feeler arm of the cockle. Two or three cockles on a long shank hook make a good sized bait that just needs a few wraps of bait elastic to secure it in place for casting.

Cockle also make a great tip off bait on the hook point below lugworms, especially blow lug.

You can force open the cockle by prising the shell apart where the two bumps are and then simply cut the cockle free of the shell by severing the muscle attached to the shell to make a neat bait.

They can be kept cool and damp in the fridge for a couple of days without problem for almost immediate use, but also freeze well removed from the shell, placed on metal trays to freeze them quickly, then placed in sealable bags, say 10 to 12 at a time. I often wrap them singly in cling film if I have time, which preserves them for longer.

CLAM

There are two types of clam. The smaller tellin clams are found in sand on sandy surf beaches and can be treated pretty much the same as cockles. Single tellin are good flatfish baits, but also work in twos and threes below lugworm as a tippet bait. These can be dug by fork, but also found in numbers washed up after storms.

The bigger mud clam found in mud banks and mud flats close to the high tide line along estuary creeks are less in number than they used to be. They leave a keyhole-shaped hole in the surface mud. They are deep and usually are a good arm's-length down, mostly, so not easy to collect.

These big clam are removed from the shell by prising them open with a knife, the flesh removed, then simply cut in to a sizeable baits and secured on the hook with bait elastic. They are a brilliant bait for bass and flounder when surf and estuary fishing.

Clam are best used fresh, but will keep alive if kept damp and cool in the fridge for a couple of days. They also freeze well, but I take them out of the shell and individually freeze each clam in a small self-sealing plastic envelope. This way I can pick and choose exactly how many I want to use at a time and minimise wastage.

There is no real season for using clams. They are a year-round bait, but again can perform best in well-coloured seas after a big sea is just starting to fine down.

RAZORFISH

Razorfish live along the very edge of the lowest low water tide line in wet but firm sand on sandy surf beaches. The sand needs to be several feet deep and without boulders or shingle for the razor to be resident. They can sometimes be found right along the full length of a beach in huge colonies, but more often than not will be only in certain areas where the sand is slow to drain and just right for them to burrow deep down in. The vertical or angled burrows can be up to three feet or more deep.

Razorfish can be collected yourself, but also bought frozen from tackle shops in packets of four to six. If collected fresh, just keep them in paper damped with seawater for a few hours and they will keep fine, or in a bucket of fresh and constantly changed seawater, for immediate fishing. Also try placing the live razorfish inside a cool box in layers on frozen ice blocks separated by a couple of layers of kitchen paper. The cold temperature helps extend the razor's life and freshness.

Longer storage requires the razorfish to be frozen. The best way

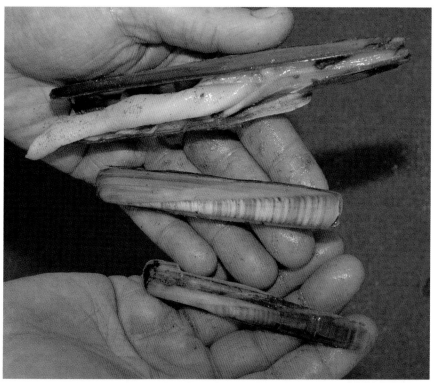

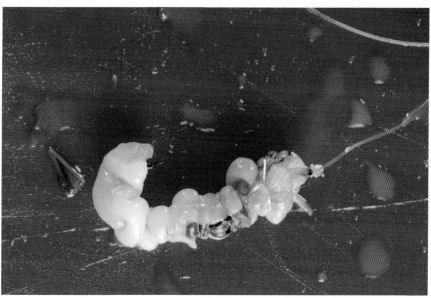

is to wrap each fresh razor individually, still in its shell, in cling film and freeze them by laying them on a metal tray that has been in the freezer for some hours. This reduces the time it takes for the razorfish to freeze. When frozen, place them in sealable sandwich bags to eliminate the chance of freezer burn, or alternatively, the plastic containers that Chinese takeaways use. Store them in say fives or tens, then you can judge how many you will need for your intended fishing session and minimise waste.

Regards presentation on the hook, razorfish can simply be pulled free from the open shell and the foot used in small sections up to two inches long for flatfish and other small species. Simply slide the razor section over the hook point and make it long enough to just slide over the eye of the hook and the tag end of the hook length knot. Now secure with a few wraps of bait elastic.

If you want to use the whole foot and surrounding flesh, especially the bigger ones for bass and cod, then a two-hook Pennel rig may be best. Again slide the whole razorfish up the first hook and well up on to the hook snood line with the foot of the razor at the hook point. Bind securely with bait elastic along the full length. Now slide the top hook in to the top of the razorfish, burying the hook shank as deep as possible to hide it.

Razor also works well as a combination bait with lugworm or ragworm. First slide the single black lug, several blow lug, or ragworm up the hook to create the right size of bait required. Now lay a whole razorfish alongside the worm and bind the whole lot together with bait elastic to form a neat, tight sausage shape. This is a particularly good bait for bass, flounder and cod, especially when storms have washed numbers of razorfish out of the sand in the autumn and winter time.

Razorfish is a very versatile bait and will catch autumn and winter cod alongside worm, but also fished on its own, especially after storms when sometimes you will find broken razorfish washing ashore after heavy seas. It is good for autumnal bass, also flounders, dabs and whiting. It is little used for thornback ray, but in early spring it can produce good results for rays when fishing sandy surf beaches.

CONCLUSION

I'm aware that there are other ways used to prolong the life of fresh bait, and the ways I have found best and described above is not definitive. However, the above works well for me and has done for over 40 years. Excessive time spent looking after bait is time I'd rather spend fishing.

Having bait available and using it at the right time in balance with nature's cycles is an essential tactic. Fish become selective and preoccupied with baits at certain times of the year, and we need to be prepared for this to maximise our catches.

When it comes to actual presentation of baits, then we've already covered many of the options, but I feel we need to clarify further a couple of points. You read in other books and in magazine articles that presentation is important. I've found presentation to matter little, except when fishing in shallow, clear water by day when fish can really inspect a bait and consider whether they actually want to eat it.

In calm, clear sea conditions, I minimise the hook length diameter, the size and type of the hook to reduce weight in the bait to retain as much natural movement as possible, and will increase the length of the hook trace, plus use ghost rigs with as many clear components as possible to minimise any visual impact. I would also use small active live baits, such as single maddie rag, or small white rag just hooked through the head end to leave the tail to wriggle freely. This natural movement can induce a take when static scent baits are completely ignored. Thin slivers of mackerel strip taken from the belly and fished on ultra-light hooks and traces can also score well in these conditions.

With any colour at all in the water, and especially at night, presentation regards the looks of the bait is wasted effort. Fish are seeking dead food by scent, pure and simple. Only scent in the water will pull fish in to that bait. They see little or nothing at night. I prefer baits that are well smashed up and secured on the hook with bait elastic designed to release the maximum amount of scent in to the water over a protracted period.

My strategy for night fishing and coloured water regards bait then is simple. Scent, and lots of it. If a fish can't first smell and follow the scent trail to source, there will be no catch. The bait needs delivering in to the fish zone, so needs to be well secured, but not excessively wrapped, with bait elastic for casting security and to keep the presentation of the hook point clear to give immediate contact with a taking fish. The bait needs to be presented tight or hard on to the seabed, for, at night, that is where the bulk of the fish are feeding. Follow that logical evaluation and you won't go far wrong!

Chapter 13:
Bite Detection

Bite detection, the actual act of seeing and interpreting a bite from a fish eating the bait, is often overlooked as a tactic, and, even more often, not fully understood, even by relatively experienced anglers. Obvious instantaneous bites that hammer the rod tip over are, in actual fact, the least likely to occur. Most bites are tentative and evolve over a few seconds, but sometimes much longer, when fish are shy or suspicious. Many anglers do not see the initial stages of a bite, only the conclusion when a fish has committed itself and fully eaten the bait, and then tried to aggressively swim away with it which finally registers on the rod tip.

With experience, good anglers can pretty much predict which species of fish has been hooked based purely on the bite characteristic that fish registered on the rod tip. Each has its own individual signature. Understanding some of the more common ones helps us hook more fish.

BITE IDENTIFICATION

Many anglers, especially when starting out sea fishing, struggle to tell what is, and isn't, a bite. It is difficult, but soon becomes obvious with a little more experience.

Common movement of the rod tip induced by wave action is a monotonous slow pull down of the rod tip, and an equally slow return of the rod tip to the original position. This is caused by wave pressure running up the line that is at an angle in the water and progressively pulling the rod tip down. As the wave reaches the point the line leaves the water, the pressure eases and the rod tip will slowly straighten. Watch the rod tip in relation to the incoming waves, and you'll see the predictability of this movement.

Weed in the water, when it first attaches to the line, may make the rod tip initially shudder, but instantly the rod tip will slowly bow down as the weight of the weed weighs on the line. This is a gradual pull down. The rod tip will now dip and lift as each wave lifts and pushes the weed in the water further up the line. Again it is predicable, monotonous and dead in its movement.

Wind on the rod tip will also make it bounce and shudder, but, if you watch this, you will see that gusts of wind induce this movement and the rod tip actually moves very little. Again it is predictable.

Bites are actually easy and obvious to see. There is no predictability about them. The rod is dead, or moving monotonously due to wave, weed or wind action, but when a fish takes it bounces erratically, pulls down in a series of rapid tugs and pulls, and, if you're lucky, rapidly hammers over and kicks back as a fish pulls the lead wires free as it makes off with the bait. It really is that simple 99 per cent of the time. Natural movement is slow and methodical; bites are rapid, fast, alive, and impossible to misinterpret.

If you're still unsure, pick the rod up and tighten the line as much as you can without pulling the grip lead free. You'll feel any bites through the line, even in rough seas and windy weather; they are that animated, aggressive and obvious.

BITE SIGNATURES
We have to understand that although fish do have individual bite characteristics, the conditions, such as the sea state, the speed of the tide, depth of water, tackle used, the size of the bait, and the distance cast will all affect the way a fish takes a bait and registers on the rod tip. What we are trying to recognise are commonalities so that we respond with the appropriate action, be that to leave the bait for the fish to fully eat it, or to respond with a quick strike to set the hook.

Flounder, if you watch the rod tip very carefully, first show as a few faint plucks or slight touches on the rod tip. This is the fish taking in the bait. These can be very gentle and often missed unless you're watching the rod tip or line just beyond the rod tip very closely. When these occur, do nothing. When the fish has the bait fully in the mouth, it will start to move away, which shows on the rod tip as three, four or five solid taps. This is usually enough to set the hook. However, I leave the rod alone until the fish gives a second series of taps, then lift the rod and wind in until I feel the weight of the lead, then pull the weight free and start to retrieve the fish.

Plaice have a similar bite, but tend to be more confident in the tapping on the rod tip after eating the bait and a decent-sized one will pull the rod tip over further on the last pull than a flounder of comparable size will. Respond only when the fish shows confidently on the rod tip.

Dabs give a series of faster taps on the rod tip. Again this indicates the fish already has the bait in the mouth and is trying to swim away. Strike

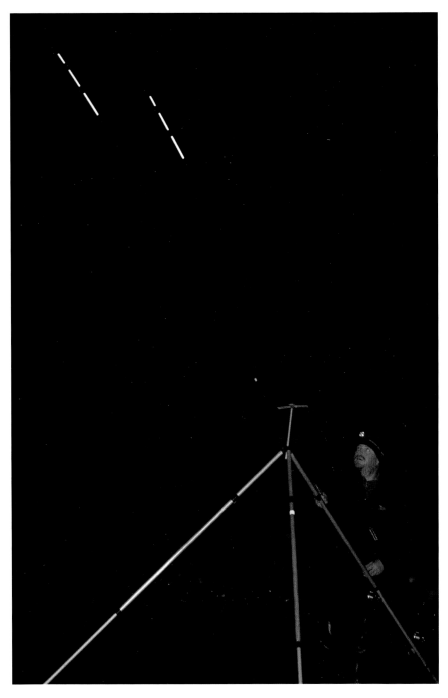

on the second set of rod tip taps. In contrast, sole tend to show with little plucks without really pulling the rod tip over to any real degree. I let sole pluck two or three times, then lift in to the fish.

Free swimming round fish, such as whiting, bass and small codling, tend to hit the bait on the run. In the case of the whiting, this shows as four to six good tugs on the rod tip as they try to continue swimming. Both codling and school bass tend to hammer the rod tip over once, followed by a series of pulls on the rod tip, again created by the hooked fish trying to swim away. Black bream from the shore give a rapid series of heavy taps on the rod tip that pulls the tip further round towards the finale of the series of taps. Again this usually indicates a well-hooked fish having come up against the weight of the lead weight and trying to bolt away.

Bigger bass can give a whole series of bite types, but the commonest are the single savage unexpected hammer over of the rod tip which springs back as the fish creates slack line. This is caused by the bass hitting the bait at speed as it swims back facing the tide. The rod needs to be lifted quickly and swept back to try to maintain a tight line, whilst also retrieving line if possible. They can also pick up a bait and run back inshore towards you. The rod tip is pulled slightly tight, then drops straight as the fish does this. Again, lift the rod, wind the reel until the line comes tight, then strike the rod upwards and backwards to fully set the hook.

Fishing at close range in to rough ground, bass can be very shy and tentative. They may only give a slight pluck on the rod tip when taking a crab bait, or you might feel a slight increase in tension on the rod tip. This is very much in a nutshell, but for anything that feels out of the ordinary: hit it, and hit it hard, to make sure the hook finds a home. You'll be surprised to see how many times what you thought was just a bit of weed hitting the line, or a small fish plucking at the bait, turns out to be a bass to be proud of.

Cod are usually targeted in rough seas, so expect a more dramatic single or double pull down of the rod tip with no prior warning. This can result in the rod tip springing back as the fish pulls the weight free, creating a little slack line, or the rod and rod rest being pulled over if the fish is swimming laterally or directly away from you and you're not paying attention. Pick up the rod and wind in any slack line as fast as you can until you feel the weight of the fish and strike hard to make sure the hook gets hold.

A ray bite is one of the hardest to interpret. In fast tides, they swim over the bait, eat it, and swim away. This sees maybe a few plucks or shuddering of the rod tip as the ray settles over the bait, then the single steady but powerful pull down of the rod tip as the ray swims off, having taken the bait. Feel the weight of the fish and strike backwards to set the hook against a tight line. In little tide pull, they can be barely noticeable settling quietly over the bait, showing only tiny trembles on the rod tip that imitate a very small fish nibbling the edges of the bait. If it is a ray, they can then sit on the bait for some time, then slowly move away pulling the rod tip, and then the rod right over until the rod rest topples too. These fish are already hooked, but lift in to the fish and let the tightening line make double sure the hook is home.

When fishing in to rough ground for bull huss, they are usually greedy and wolf down the bait, which sees the rod tip show a series of pulls and knocks. Leave these until the fish tries to swim away with the bait and is fully pulling over the rod tip. Strike these bites hard, as a huss has a tough mouth that hooks find hard to penetrate.

When after wrasse, you will normally be fishing a tight line for them and pretty much at fairly close range in front of you. These can be two different bites. The easy one is a single savage dip of the rod as the wrasse snatches the bait, which needs to be struck quickly and hard. The other is a few rapid taps, which again need to be hit quickly and firmly. Wrasse, if some of the bait is left intact, can return for a second go, as the bait is dropped back if you miss the first strike.

Conger eels can be the trickiest of all. They are sensitive feeders for the most part and can often take a bait without registering at all on the rod tip. You only realise they are hooked when you retrieve to re-bait. However, a typical conger bite is usually one of two things. You see the rod tip individually tap very lightly a few times. This is the conger taking in the bait. This may happen two or three times, it depends on the size of the bait and the size of the conger. Bigger conger take their time. Do nothing! You then get one or two sharper tugs that pull the rod tip down a few inches. If the eel feels the hook, they can just sit there pondering what to do. If they don't, they move off, dragging the rod tip over. This is luck and judgement time. If you think an eel is playing possum, release a few feet of line and watch for the line pulling tight again. This little bit of slack can fool the conger into a false sense of security and it will move away, showing on the rod tip as a steady continual pull down. If nothing happens, give it more slack and wait. Only hit the fish when it shows some commitment to pulling the rod tip over. When it does, strike hard and hold the fish to stop it reaching any nearby snags.

If you're lucky enough to target shore tope, then these, too, need a little thought regards the strike. Tope, in calm weather and daylight, can pick a bait up, run, drop the bait, come back and pick it up again. Sometimes, if its smaller pack tope in a group, it may be a different fish that picks up the bait the second time. If they continually keep dropping the bait, when this happens, retrieve a few feet of line slowly. This can force the tope to grab the bait and fully run with it in fear of another tribe member beating them to it. It will gulp the bait in as it swims, so wait a few seconds as line peels off the reel, then sweep the rod backwards and high to hit the fish. If a tope just grabs the static bait while swimming at speed, and keeps running with the bait, wait until the run starts to slow, then strike. When the run slows, it is the tope gulping back the bait. This strike method helps avoid deeply hooked fish.

When working surface popping and shallow diving plugs for bass, I have a theory that they use their hard, bony heads to head-butt prey on the first attack in an attempt to stun it, making it easier to grab and swallow the second time around. I think this could explain, partly, why so many bass are foul hooked on lures. If a bass attacks a lure and you feel the hit but there is no hook up, just keep working the lure, but with a long pause immediately after the hit, and the likelihood is that the bass will attack again as the lure is static.

Those were a few of the more common signature bites then. Try to learn some of these characteristics and you'll soon be able to predict which fish is taking the bait, and choose the best course of action to hook it, but always keep an open mind, as fish, on the day, can and will surprise you.

IMPROVING BITE DETECTION AT THE ROD TIP

Getting bites is one thing; you need to be able to clearly see them too. For night fishing, many rods are sold with simply painted tips, usually white, orange, or yellow. White is ok, yellow is ok, orange is pretty poor in comparison. Paint, though, is generally poor and needs strong direct light to illuminate the rod tip, either via a headlight or background lamp.

Far more effective is reflective tape sold to reflect headlights off the back of trailers and caravans. This picks up the slightest light value and reflects it back, even when the light source is angled well away from the tape. It can also be viewed a long way away from the rod tips if you wander off to see how another angler is getting on. This needs to be applied lengthways between the intermediate rings and should be at least 24 inches long. Adding short lengths of tape a few inches long at the tip is not enough. Consider rods of 12 feet plus in length, raised on an extendable-height rod rest and the tip will be at least 15 feet up in the air. The added length of tape makes seeing small bites far easier.

White reflective tape is best, but yellow is also good. The red can play tricks with your eyes, many find, so judge this one yourself.

Taped-on rod tip lights are popular, but are not great if you are a powerful caster. I mention these as an option as modern LED type lights do show bites clearly, but for me I prefer the reflective tape.

LINE CHOICE

As good and as popular as monofilament line is, it is generally stretchy and therefore disguises and waters down bite registration at the rod tip. The further you cast, the worse the situation gets. To partially combat this, obviously choose line brands with less stretch and load with as lighter breaking strain as you can get away with over the type of ground you are fishing. Make sure you fish the line as tight as you can to a release wire grip lead when at range to maintain as much bite detection through the line as possible.

For close to medium range fishing, say up to about 75 yards and when bass fishing, using Fluorocarbon as a main line is a good option. It has less stretch than mono, so transfers information up the line to the rod tip much better. The down side, in my opinion, is that it does not cast as well as the softer mono, Fluorocarbon is stiffer in character and less predictable coming off the reel spool, plus is prone to lifting during mid cast. Advances are never ending regards Fluorocarbon though, and the issue of stiffness is slowly being worked on, so keep pace with developments and watch this line as a better option over time.

Not necessarily the best for fishing in all situations, and it is only really practical for fixed spool reels (spinning reels), but the best for bite detection by far is braid line. This has virtually no stretch, so even at range whatever happens at the hook end is pretty much directly transferred to the rod tip, magnifying even the slightest of bites. Its slimmer diameter for the same given breaking strain compared to mono also means it catches less tide pressure and minimises bow in the line that also massively contributes to poor bite detection, especially in windy weather or fast lateral tide runs.

A technological advancement in line also needs to be mentioned here. The famous company Berkley, based in the USA, introduced a forward thinking line at the edge of technology called Nanofil back in 2011. This is made from 100 per cent Dyneema, an incredibly strong fibre. A special heat process sees around 300 of these small individual fibres bonded together to form one very supple line that is thin in diameter, has little if any stretch, but with a smooth surface that increases casting distance, due to less spool and rod ring friction, and air drag, by a noticeable margin. It offers incredible bite detection at ultra-long range and offers a viable alternative to braid for both beach casting and for spinning and working lures. It deserves a special mention as I see more and more technology being applied to line, advancing line performance regards casting, abrasion and bite detection in the medium term from the publication of this book.

ROD REST DESIGN

One of the most important items of tackle for bite detection is an adjustable rod rest with telescopic legs. Fishing short, single length rod rests puts you at a huge disadvantage as you cannot fully adapt to the weather and sea conditions to maximise bite detection.

All three legs of the rod rest should be height-adjustable. If you are on uneven ground, such as a rock ledge, this gives you the option to set each leg height individually to suit the uneven ground feature and get the rod rest head dead level to allow the rods to fish efficiently. The extendable legs also allow the rod rest head to be adjusted for height to an ideal maximum of 8 feet, or a little more. At this full height, the legs have a wide footprint on even ground and sand which dramatically increases its overall stability when using longer rods in excess of 13 feet in length.

The rod rest should also be fitted with an adjustable for height rod cup bar. This supports the rods higher on the rod rest to gain tip height, but also keep the rods, and reels, well away from surging surf and swells.

Using the full adjustable leg height, and the adjustable rod butt bar, you can get the tip of a typical 14-foot rod up to 18 feet up off the ground. This means that in a heavy surf your line is entering the water further out, limiting wave action on the line and avoiding the worst of the weed, which destroys bite detection. Anglers with typical short rod rests that stand only five feet high or less once opened, and sport no adjustable rod cup bar, only give a maximum rod tip height of the length of the rod. Also, the short rod rests are totally unstable and need added weight to hold them down when fishing two rods in windy weather with a heavy surf action. Standard short rod rests, then, are grossly inefficient, and will see you capitulate to bad weather and go home empty-handed, whereas the angler with the bigger adjustable more versatile rod rest will fish on regardless.

IDEAL ROD ANGLE FOR IMPROVED BITE DETECTION

Rod angle in relation to the sea in varying conditions is a major factor in seeing bites clearly. Get it wrong and it becomes almost impossible to decipher bites from common wave and weed action.

In heavy seas and with a strong wind blowing pretty much straight at you, the rod is best placed as high as is practical in the rod rest, facing directly towards the sea and inclined at a 25-degree angle. The rod tip may dip slowly as a wave runs up the line, but bites from decent sized fish will be instantly seen. False bites from wave action and weed will be minimised.

In a lighter sea with an even pattern of surf tables and the wind nothing more than a breeze, but again fairly straight on to the beach, the rod tip can be lowered in height and positioned at an angle of 45 degrees. This brings the angle of the line as it enters the sea shallower, keeping the line tighter and straighter in relation to the lead weight to maximise bite detection.

If there is a strong side wind blowing, then turn the rod rest and rods to face away from the direction the wind is blowing so that they are lateral to the sea's edge. This sees the bow in the line created by the wind more in line with the rod tip. I also like to drop the rods to a shallower angle of between 50 and 60 degrees, with the aim to keep the line as shallow in angle as possible in relation to the cast out lead weight, but still be above the inner waves that break ashore to limit wave pull on the rod tip that covers up small bites. Readjusting the rod rest leg heights, but keeping the rear leg long, has the effect of dropping the rod rest head and the rod tips without compromising overall stability.

In flat calm seas, I have the rod rest legs at their lowest height, but keep the rear leg long to fully drop the height of the rod rest bar, and again position the rest parallel with the sea's edge. I do not use the rod cup bar in these conditions, preferring to rest the rod butts on the ground. The rods face away from any wind, but the tips are positioned as low as I can get them to the water with the line as shallow as possible to maintain that vitally important straight tight line to the lead weight. Some anglers still like their rod tips angled towards the sea in these calm conditions, but it is not as sensitive as the side-on approach.

ROD TIP DESIGN

The rod tip design you fish with also has a great bearing on seeing and deciphering bites. In very calm weather, you can use a very soft almost quiver-type tip, and, if fishing to a tight line, you will see even the tiniest of bites, especially at close to medium range when using braided line. Some of the longer 15-feet rods with soft tips can still be cast in excess of 125 yards and show up bites incredibly well in flat seas.

However, in rougher seas, soft tips will move too much, this being caused by wave and weed action on the line, making it impossible to identify bites. In rougher seas, a stiffer-tipped rod is better as it does not react so easily to weed and wave and is more predictable in its natural movement. But when a fish, even a small dab at long range, rattles the bait, this will be easily seen on the rod tip.

Having the option of both rod types is best, but if you only have the one option, go for the stiffer tip every time, as it will still work in calm seas, but is better-adapted to heavy seas, weed and wave action, which the soft rod tip type cannot cope with.

Chapter 14:
Tactics, Tips,
Tricks

All too often when shore fishing, it is the little things you do that change your fortunes on the day. This chapter puts together a few of the tactics, tips and tricks I've learnt the hard way over many, many years. Some I've found out myself, others I've gleaned from other anglers. They are simple things to do and try, but they can make a massive difference.

FISH TWO RODS
When beach fishing, I always fish two rods, side by side in the rod rest. I use identical rods, reels and load with identical line and shock leader. The only difference may be the type of rig I choose to fish with.

Fishing two rods tends to see them react to the wind and wave conditions exactly the same. I can compare the two rod tips side by side. If one rod tip registers a movement and the other does not, this indicates a potential bite and forewarns something different is happening and warrants close attention. So often, over the years, this very scenario has seen me hovering over the rod, waiting and willing it to pull over, and more often than not it does, resulting in a faster strike reaction from me that I feel increases my chances of hooking more fish.

There is a more important reason I fish two rods side by side. When I start fishing, I tend to cast one rod as far as I possibly can. The other I will cast shorter to, say, middle distance. I make a mental note of which rod is getting the most bites over the next few casts, and if it's the longer range rod I start casting the middle distance rod longer. If neither rod catches, then I cast the longer one slightly shorter and the middle distance one slightly longer narrowing the band the two rigs are fishing apart until I get bites. This simple ploy lets me establish the exact area and distance out from the tide line the majority of fish are feeding in. If this latter approach does not work either, then I cast one rod short and the second just short of middle distance. Again I note bites and will draw the two rigs on future casts closer together until I again find where the fish are feeding. This means I'm covering the maximum amount of ground and inevitably find exactly where the bulk of fish are located.

Another benefit with fishing two rods is that you can fish a big bait at range for rays and cod maybe, but drop in shorter with a two- or three-hook rig targeting smaller whiting, flatfish, and anything else that is swimming by to enjoy a good mixed catch session. This guarantees you some active sport, but with the chance of a big fish happening along too. Alternatively, you can fish two big baits at range to double your chances of a bigger fish, or fish close in for flounder and the like, and at long range for dabs with smaller baits.

The obvious advantage in fishing two rods is that it literally doubles your chances of fish, but the reality is that when fishing both rods with, say, a three-hook rig, you have six baits in the water, compared to the

angler fishing just the one rod who only has three chances. Simple maths, but over a month, year and lifetime, the difference in the numbers and species of fish caught will be huge.

Only in very bad weather and heavy seas will I cut down to fish just one rod. In these conditions, with weed in the water, concentrating on just one will pay dividends as your concentration rate will be much higher and the loss of time sorting problems out minimised. When bass fishing, it is essential to hold the rod and feel for bites whether you are surf fishing, or fishing in to rough ground. Instant strike reaction is the key to consistent bass fishing. Rods in rod rests will see a good proportion of bass bites missed.

THE LINE-BACK TECHNIQUE
The line-back technique has been employed by anglers for well over 100 years, but still has its place today. It was developed around the turn of the 20th century to allow anglers to fish at long range on very shallow beaches. It was a popular method especially in Mid Wales, Morecambe Bay, and on the Lincolnshire beaches where the tide can ebb out several hundred yards over what is pretty much flat, featureless sand. Anglers in East Anglia also adopted it to maximise their catches of cod from low water and through the early flood tide during the bigger spring tides.

The basic technique is simple, and hasn't changed much, but we'll look at it through 21st century eyes.

Taking tackle first, the longer European style beachcasters casting four to six ounces and with a length of 15 to 16 feet are perfect. They will give you maximum casting distance without the need for off-the-ground or full pendulum casting, which tend to be used by the more experienced angler, and in this situation will only gain you a relatively short distance in terms of what lining back can do.

The only reel for this type of fishing, at least to get the maximum effect, is a large 8000 size fixed spool reel. The best reels are the ones that come with a standard deep profile mono spool. This will hold way more line than a shallow spool designed to take only braid. To get maximum line capacity you can fill a standard spool with 20-pound mono, and an 8000 reel should hold around 400 yards of this typically 0.40-millimetre diameter line. This should be just about enough for most line back situations. However, the alternative is to load a third to half of the spool with 20-pound mono, then top shot with 20- to 30-pound braid. This will give you somewhere in the region of up to 600 yards plus of available line and cover you pretty much anywhere in the UK.

Braid line is the best choice because it does not stretch much. This puts you in more direct contact with the fish at long range and will dramatically improve your bite detection ability. Also, having a much smaller diameter for the same breaking strain in comparison to mono, it does not suffer as much from tide drag on the line. The straighter the line is in the water, the better your bite detection will be. Using 40- to 50-pound braid will see the line with enough strength to dispense with a shock leader as most braids break well over their quoted breaking strain.

You still need to add a shock leader when fishing mono main line, so go with a 60-pound mono shock leader for casting weights up to six ounces. Use a clear mono leader in daylight, but a coloured leader helps at night because you can see the end tackle or fish coming towards you in your headlight beam.

The actual method is simple. You wade out as far as you can, then cast normally, but as far as possible. As the tide floods in and gets to lower thigh level, open the bale-arm of the reel and, while walking slowly backwards, release line but keep it just tight to the lead by letting it flip through a semi-closed hand. Walk backwards until you are in ankle-deep water, then stay there until the water reaches your lower thigh again. You keep retreating like this, a bit at a time, as long as you can, releasing line and leaving the baits where they were initially cast. This leaves them in ever deepening water until a fish finds them.

If you are fishing two or three hooks, when you get a bite, do not strike. Let the fish take the bait, then wait. The activity of the first fish will often bring another one in to investigate. This especially applies to flatfish and whiting, but also cod, which often come through in small groups. With experience, you will come to learn the difference when first one, then two, then three fish hook themselves.

The traditional line-back method often employed heavier eight-ounce sinkers to guarantee the bait stayed there, but normal modern five- to six-ounce grip leads with the wires crimped down to increase release pressure work well enough. Obviously bigger fish, such as cod and rays, will pull the weight out and these fish need to be played and retrieved as normal.

In the course of lining back, you might find yourself 400 yards or more away from where your bait is actually fishing.

You can see the advantage lining back gives you. If you were casting from the water's edge, even a good caster on a good day with a following wind would struggle to fish at even 150 yards. By lining back, you at least double this, and more. Keeping the bait in the deeper water for as long as possible maximises your chances of hitting fish that are reluctant to move in to very shallow water. On the flat beaches it also gives you a much better chance of catching fish like thornback rays and bigger cod that again will rarely venture in to just a couple of feet of water. Often these fish are present on the shallow beaches, it's just that the anglers conventionally casting do not have the range to reach them.

Lining-back, then, is a very effective method that allows you to fish very shallow beaches that normally would not produce much with conventional casting tactics.

A couple of points to bear in mind. Always travel light with just a few spare hooks and rigs, leader and bait. It's obviously also useful if you wear chest waders. On the flatter shallower beaches, once the tide starts to flood it can race in at walking speed on the spring tides, so it's best to leave your gear and rod rest well above the tide line and hold the rod, feeling for bites. Alternatively, use a push-in monopod to put the rod in, which is easier to walk back with, and lighter in weight to carry.

FISHING THE ARC
The standard way of fishing for most beach anglers is to fish a static bait anchored to the seabed by a release wire lead. This is a good way of catching fish...most of the time. It lets itself down, though, when bites are few and far between, when fish are lethargic and reluctant to work up a baits scent trail, and when fish are thin on the ground and concentrated individually or in small groups.

There is a more mobile tactic, though, called 'fishing the arc', that can get you a few bites when everything else fails.

One thing to be aware of is that if bites are generally slow, then casting out to long range probably won't see a swift improvement in catches. It's worth a try, but often fails. The food, and the fish, are more likely to be in the surf tables where the surf action is constantly scouring out the sand.

To begin, we need to change the wired lead for a plain lead. The choice of weight needs to be adjusted so that it is just heavy enough to be moved by wave and lateral tidal pressure on the line. The speed of travel of the weight must be occasional and gradual. The best weight shapes for this type of fishing are the round watch type leads, or small torpedo-shaped bombs.

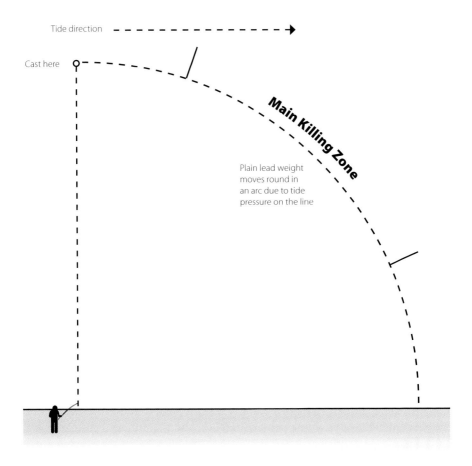

Tide direction

Cast here

Main Killing Zone

Plain lead weight
moves round in
an arc due to tide
pressure on the line

Imagine standing facing the surf and looking straight in front of you. If the tide is moving left to right, in your mind's eye, imagine a cone or quarter circle shape drawn from where you intend to cast back round until it dissects a line drawn at a 90-degree angle to the right from your feet. This is the 'fishing arc'. The accompanying diagram illustrates this cone shape, so there is no need to worry too much about angles and degrees.

Within this arc is a killing zone when the likelihood of a bite is that much greater. This 'zone' lies between 20 degrees and 70 degrees off the imaginary line straight in front of you where you cast to. If you don't get a bite within this specific zone, then your chances diminish quickly as the weight travels closer to the 90-degree line drawn to the right of your feet.

To fish the arc, aim to cast out in a slightly downtide direction, and at about 10 degrees to the right of the imaginary line drawn straight in front of you. This slight angle on the cast will help apply early tide and wave pressure to the line and get the lead weight moving in the right direction.

Standing upright, point the rod tip down and directly at where you cast the weight and watch the line. You will feel the weight start to gradually move around and a bow form in the line. As it does so, keep an almost tight line. Even with mono, because you are fishing at relatively short range, say no more than 70 yards or so, you will literally feel the weight moving and sliding over ripples in the sand and across small pebbly areas. If you are using braid line, and you'll need to fish a pretty light lead with this due to its thinner diameter, then you will feel every little change in the seabed contours. By keeping the line almost tight, and watching the bow in the line, you will also see when the weight stops and starts moving again.

By having the bait gradually moving, your bait is now covering much more ground, and therefore stands a greater chance of coming across a fish that is fairly static on the seabed and not actively searching for food. Seeing a moving bait come close to it is often enough to trigger an otherwise disinterested fish in to biting.

This arc method of fishing will also locate any slightly deeper holes or gutters present. The weight rolls in to these and stops. You will naturally feel this happen. If you choose the weight of your lead weight correctly, the light tidal pressure is not enough to lift the weight up the incline of the hole. Fish often lie in these holes and scoured-out areas, waiting for food to get washed in to them by the tide, so this arc method imitates this perfectly. It pays to leave the bait in the hole for a minute or two, then retrieve a few feet of line to lift the weight out of the hole and get it moving again.

By maintaining an almost tight line, and watching the line bow, you will first see the bow straighten and dart forward quickly (it is an obvious unnatural movement), then a split second later feel the pull of a fish through the rod in your hands as it takes the bait. Do not strike immediately; let the fish pull again before lifting the rod to feel the weight of the fish and begin reeling it in.

Because the fish are not necessarily feeding, drop down the size of the bait and hook to further increase the chance of bites. Small one-inch sections of lugworm or ragworm, or a couple of maddie rag nicked on the end of a size 6 Aberdeen, are all you need. For sea trout, try a small sliver of mackerel belly about one and a half inches long, which also happens to be a good winter flounder bait too.

It can also pay to reduce your hook snood breaking strain down to just ten pounds when fishing in daylight, which is ample for the species being targeted. Clear mono, or better still Fluorocarbon, in this diameter moves better in the water and gives a more natural presentation, plus the fish find thinner line more difficult to see. Make your hook snoods about 18 inches long to make the bait move more.

The arc method is very effective for flounders, dabs, plaice, whiting, rockling, small turbot, school bass, coalfish and sea trout, also golden-grey mullet. Surprise rays, such as small-eyed ray, also happen along and will take a small bait in preference to a normal ray bait. It works at any time of year, and is what match anglers and experienced pleasure anglers call a 'blank breaker'.

UPTIDE SHORE CASTING

A strong left-to-right, or right-to-left side-on wind is one of the most difficult situations for a beach angler to combat. When you cast, the wind creates a large downwind bow in the line which destroys bite detection and increases the target area for any floating weed present to collect on the line. There is a way, though, that you can minimise the effects of this and fish much more effectively.

To combat this, walk uptide of your fishing position about 30 yards or so, more if the wind is especially strong, then make your normal cast straight out to sea letting the lead settle. With the rod tip held high and the line fairly tight, now walk back to your rod rest releasing some line, but keeping just in contact with the lead weight. When you get back to your rod rest, wind in any slack and you will see that your line leaves the rod tip heading pretty much straight out to sea. Effectively you have created an uptide bow in the line and this will help the lead weight grip for far longer. The bow in the line now sees the line pulling more directly on the anchored lead and acts just like an anchor line pulling the weight deeper in to the seabed. Also, because the line is in more of a straight line to the anchored lead weight, bite detection is improved. Bites tend to show with the bent rod tip straightening as a fish takes the bait and pulls the lead weight out. It's then a case of winding in line until you feel weight, and striking to make sure the hook is fully home.

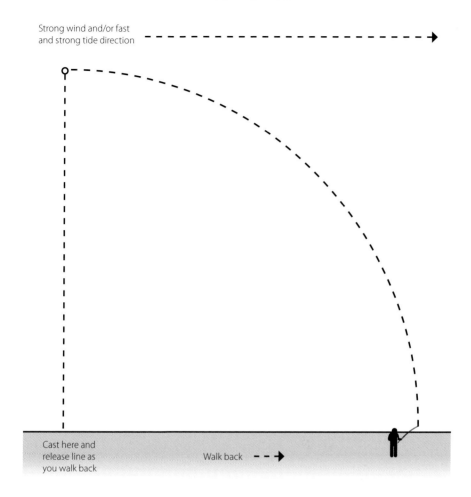

Strong wind and/or fast
and strong tide direction

Cast here and
release line as
you walk back

Walk back

This also works equally well with a strong lateral tidal current. If you walk uptide towards the oncoming current, again between 30 and 50 yards, make the cast as before and walk back to your original position. Release a little line initially to create a bow, then, when you return to your fishing spot, wind in any major slack line, and again the line from the rod tip will now be straight out in front of you, but the bow in the line will help pull the grip wired weight deep in to the sand and hold it firm.

If you normally fish five-ounce lead weights, then, to cover this situation, also have a couple of six-ounce weights with extra-long grip wires fitted with you. The heavier weight and longer wires will dig in even more and keep you fishing longer.

This simple uptiding technique will keep you fishing effectively in any difficult side-on conditions. If you cast conventionally, straight out in front of you in this situation, almost instantly the lateral tide or wind will bow the line downtide of your fishing station and quickly pull the lead weight free.

TIPS & TRICKS

Bite detection is not all about watching the rod tip. There are specific situations when watching a slightly slack line is far more explanatory of what is happening at the hook end. The following is a good way to fish in calm or near-calm conditions with a gentle wave pattern, or when fishing an area of less disturbed water, such as an estuary channel, side creek, or eddy.

After casting, tighten the line to the lead weight as normal. Now release no more than a couple of feet of line, just enough to create a small downward bow or belly in the line. Natural sea and wind movement will slightly lift the line in a gentle predictive fashion. But watch carefully, and when a fish takes, the line will tighten and straighten suddenly in a much more animated fashion, then fall back in to the bow. It's an obvious fish bite. Having slack line, especially when fishing at close range, guarantees that the bait is tight to the seabed; also, the fish has a little room to take the bait before feeling the line pressure and moving away. A simple trick that helps catch fish when tight line tactics fail.

Adding a float bead on to the hook length just above a small bait helps give the bait lift and movement in the water. You need to choose a float bead, or use two float beads in line, to match the size of the bait you want to fish. One bead is enough for single maddie rag, but bigger beads, depending on size, are needed for slightly larger baits. The distance away from the hook that the float bead is positioned can be crucial. With this in mind, I like to fix my float beads in place by putting a sliding stop knot or rubber stop knot either side of the bead. The flat bead can then be repositioned easily, either closer to the hook, or further away. I usually start with a distance of about eight inches between the bead and the bait to give the bait some movement. The closer the bead is to the hook and the shorter the hook length, the less movement the bait will have. If you try to balance the bait so that it lifts and drops on to the seabed as the float beads tries to lift it, this is ideal. Float beads work well for a wide variety of species, but especially black bream, flatfish and golden-grey mullet.

Adding alternately coloured rig beads above a hook in daylight and

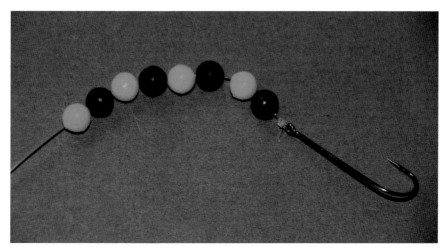

clearish seas can also attract fish in to the bait. These can be single colours in banks of three or four, or, better still, in mixed colours that are more distinctive. You'll find some bead combination colours work best for different species. For plaice, an alternate mix of green and black beads in a bank of six can be deadly. Plaice also take well on baits below red and white, or red and yellow beads. Flounder prefer blue and white, or red and white combinations. Pink and white is a good colour combo for small surf turbot, but again will take plaice and flounder too. To make the beads work to their full extent, use a flat shaped lead weight, and occasionally twitch the lead back towards you a few inches every minute or so. It makes the beads move and lift and will draw the eye of any inert, disinterested fish and can induce an attack.

Also try mixing coloured beads with a central float bead. Choose a float bead size that will just lift the bait when a wave moves over it when in shallow water to give an otherwise inert bait some natural movement. This is a good trick to try when bites are hard to come by in shallow, gin-clear seas and fishing in daylight.

Luminous beads are also worth trying at night, especially in slightly coloured or deep water. The best colour is a luminous green. Fish one small bead in front of a small bait targeting dabs, whiting and flounder. For bigger baits intended for cod and codling, also rough ground ling, rockling and conger, fish two or three 5-millimetre luminous green beads directly above the hook. A good tip is to charge these before casting by holding the beads in the beam of your headlight, or rapidly charge them by using the flash on a camera or phone.

If you want to guarantee a smallish bait is fishing right on the seabed in rougher surf tables, or in a lateral tide current, nip one or two small BB-sized non-toxic split shot on to the hook length just above the hook. This gives enough weight to keep a small bait anchored down but still moving over the seabed naturally.

This is a neat trick using a wishbone hook trace to stimulate small fish to feed. Form a 10-inch loop in the end of a hook trace by tying in a double overhand knot. Cut the loop line once to create two loose ends, one about 14 inches long and the shorter about 6 inches in length. To the shorter trace, tie on a size 2/0 to 3/0 hook and bait with a large piece of peeler crab, whole lugworm, or short fillet section of mackerel etc. To the longer hook trace, tie on a smaller size 2, 4 or 6 hook and bait with a much smaller piece of the same bait, or even a different bait. This has the effect of maximising the smell from the bigger bait to draw the fish in, but offers it a smaller piece of bait that looks like it has broken off the main bit and is easy to eat. Using a different bait gives another option, but it still maximises the scent trail to initially pull the fish in within range of the baits. Again a tactic to remember when fish are not available in numbers and widely spread. You'll often find bigger fish eat the small bait first, then immediately the bigger bait as well with both hooks set in the mouth when the fish is landed.

In bad weather and fast tides, you can get release wire grip leads to hold better by wrapping an elastic band around the nose over the wires. Put the loop of the band over a set wire, wrap the elastic band fairly tightly around the fixed wires and nose of the lead, and finally loop the end over another wire to secure it. When you pull hard on the line the wires will spring forward and pull off the band. It's a cheap but effective trick if you haven't got any bigger leads with you.

You can get better presentation in both a mono and Fluorocarbon hook length if you run the line over your knee a few times to put a little heat in to it. This softens and straightens the line and aids bait presentation in the water.

When beach casting, imagine the ground in front of you as being a big fan shape. Use the full width of the fan, covering it with both long and short casts. If you take notice, you will see that certain areas produce a lot more bites. This will be a shallow channel, scoured out hole, or some other feature that will concentrate the fish. Explore and search every bit of ground to find the hotspots.

Each time you remove old bait from a hook prior to re-baiting, make sure you throw the old bait in to the water at the water's edge. This acts

like a groundbait and will wash out to sea a few yards with the undertow. Let a little time pass and drop a baited rig just ten yards out in front of you. This little dodge has hooked me many many fish that I otherwise would not have caught.

When fishing an estuary channel, it can be a mistake to cast out in to the middle channel. This middle section may see fish passing through, but not really stopping to feed. You'll be far more successful if you stand and look along the bank you are stood on, and cast at an angle a few yards seaward so that your baits are fishing on the incline of the channel sides. This is where the majority of fish sit, such as flounder, and where bass will hunt as they travel in with the tide. Also fish the incline by casting in a fan shape further and further out with each cast so that you cover as much ground as possible. After a half dozen casts or so, move down another 20 yards and repeat fan casting. This also works when using lures for estuary and rough ground bass.

Flashing a bright headlight across the water is enough to scare off bass and other fish working very tight inshore. To reduce the light output of a headlight, try adding a red lens made from cut-out see-through plastic over the light lens and tape it in position. Red will really diffuse the amount of light emitted from the headlight, but still give you more than enough to work with for baiting up etc. Many torches now offer several light outputs, low to high; ideal for baiting up on low, but good on high for seeing long range. Some even do a red option as standard, so check this out when you buy a headlamp.

For beach and standard rough ground and rock ledge fishing, make sure you buy the best-quality headlamp you can afford. For beach work choose one with a large round pool of light that illuminates as much ground around you as possible. This enables you to work effectively within your fishing station, but also has the power and width of light to locate fish in the surf prior to landing. For rock ledge fishing I prefer a headlight that has a powerful, long range beam that can illuminate lobster pots up to 100 yards away and help me pick my way down cliff paths in the dark if need be. Reliability is the other essential, and cheap LED lights might be ok on a beach with easy access off should they fail, but it's too much of a risk from the safety angle and downright foolhardy when fishing the rock ledges. I also carry a spare small headlight as back up, just in case of problems.

When fishing the rock ledges for big fish, such as tope and conger, I carry two lanyards with small, strong, lightweight carabineers on that connect to stainless steel wire rock nuts that the climbers use to jam in to cracks in the rock. Once secured in a rock crack, these, and the lanyard tied round my rod rest legs, stops big fish dragging the rod rest over and damaging the rods. It also keeps the rod rest secure in a side wind and a heavy sea swell.

In my tackle box, I carry a few lengths of various diameter plastic tubing, silicone tube sleeving, a few lengths of 18-millimetre stainless steel wire, a little soft telephone wire, insulation tape, and other odds and ends. I also carry a pair of long-nosed pliers. These 'bits' can be used to make up small items of tackle, such as booms and clips, should a situation occur that warrants some inventive thinking. They can also be pressed in to service to make basic repairs to tackle and rod rest if needed.

SAFETY

We need to consider safety too. Always make sure someone at home knows exactly where you will be and when to expect you home. Make a point of calling home the minute you reach the safety of the car and inform of your impending return. It confirms all is well, and puts family member's minds at rest.

Do not rely on mobile phones, as in many areas fishing marks are remote and mobile signals are intermittent at best, and often just not available.

Ideally fish in pairs, and absolutely so when working deep water rock ledges. Never take silly chances when trying to land even big fish. Think before you act!

Sea anglers do not help rescue workers by wearing dark, drab clothing. Make sure you wear at least a coat that is in a bright red or yellow colour that can be visually picked out against normal beach or cliff terrain. Talking to rescue officials, this is a real issue for them and has cost sea anglers lives in the past.

Chapter 15:
Time & Motion
Fishing

In modern life, none of us have enough time. It is a precious commodity that we can ill afford to waste and squander. It is the same when fishing. If you want to be a successful and consistent angler, then time must become your friend. You must learn to maximise what time you have and make it as productive as possible.

Never underestimate how efficient fishing increases your ability to catch fish. The longer you have a bait in the water, logic dictates you inevitably must catch more fish. It is an obvious and simple rule, but one that is crucial. Yet stand on a beach, rock ledge, or pier and watch what most anglers do, and the actual time they have a bait in the water in relation to their actual time spent fishing lays somewhere between 30 per cent and 60 per cent of the time. The other 40 per cent is totally wasted effort.

We're going to look at how, using time and motion related to fishing, we can maximise our time with bait in the water, and minimise waste by being ultra-efficient. In business, efficient practice limits mistakes, increases production, and maximises profits. Though fishing for fun as an individual is not a business, we are still looking for an end result, and in that we need to be workmanlike in our approach.

OUT OF HOURS PREPARATION

Laziness is the weakness we have to guard against. Some anglers choose to make rigs up as they go along on the beach, rocks or pier. You can see that being adaptive might be necessary sometimes, but the fact is that this shows a lack of preparation, which wastes a huge chunk of fishing time. You should have an idea exactly what rig types you need to be carrying to suit the majority of fishing situations and have at least six of each already prepared, so that if you lose one or two, you still have a ready supply to continue with.

What I did in my early years, and still do today, is sit either in front of the TV, or at my desk, and tie up spare rigs at home when fishing is not an option. In this way you build up a good selection and can at least carry most options in a rig wallet to cover any common situation you come across in normal fishing. That said, to save time and weight, when going to a specific venue for a specific species, I only carry the rigs applicable to the target fish and venue.

Used rigs I tend to put in the cool box after fishing, then wash these in warm water when I get home. Before fishing next, I'll check over the rigs for abrasion and weakness, change hook lengths for new, and replace the hooks ready for the next time.

In my shed, I keep trays of leads, separated by size and type. I only carry what I know is needed for actual fishing, but have a large stock of weights at home so that I can instantly replace lost ones prior to any trip. This may sound petty, but all too often anglers leave making or buying leads to the last minute, then find they cannot be replaced in time when wanting to go fishing and have to compromise.

After each trip, I fully check over my rods. These will have been washed in clean, warm water immediately after I return home, but I now pay particular attention to the rod ring liners and check for any cracks or chips by rubbing my finger inside the inserts, which will pick up any anomalies. No point spending money on fuel to get to a mark, then walking a fair way, only to find a rod is carrying a broken ring. This is a common occurrence for many anglers, but just a few seconds spent checking eliminates the problem. I still carry a spare tip ring, the tube ready filled with hot melt glue, in my box or bag, though, in case I suffer a breakage while fishing.

I do the same with my reels. These are washed and left to dry as soon as I get home from fishing to minimise the chance of any corrosion. So many anglers don't do this, just putting their reels in their box and bag, never washing them, then finding they don't work properly the next time they get to the beach. I re-oil the bearings in my reels after three trips, and fully strip and service the reel after a dozen trips or so – even sooner if I feel performance is dropping away.

I also check the main line. This you can do easily by having an empty old reel at home, running the line off through a damp kitchen towel to clean it of salt while checking for any nicks and abrasions, then re-spool the line on to the original fishing reel. I also check and re-tie shock leaders at home. Yes, you'll occasionally need to tie new leaders while fishing, but it's sensible to start with reliable or new ones from the off.

Again, on getting home, headlamps and camp lights are recharged and checked for any obvious problems. I also clean the lenses on headlamps to remove salt film and maintain maximum light output.

The rod rest also gets periodical attention. A good clean with warm freshwater to remove salt, then re-oil all the moving parts. I once watched an angler setting up alongside me, and when he tried to open one of the forward legs on his rod rest, it was so stiff with corrosion and grime that the connection snapped. He went home without making a single cast!

I've learnt to be meticulous, too, checking zips on clothing for corrosion, sharpening bait knives after each trip, washing bait cloths out, cleaning out the cool box, and very simple things like making sure fishing clothes are washed, dried and ready for the next time. I never leave anything to the last minute!

This serves a secondary, equally important purpose too, in that, preparing for each trip individually, I'm less likely to leave important tackle items and rigs behind. It's a form of self-assessment that increases my overall efficiency.

There is also a confidence issue here. You're looking forward to fishing, then when you get there, you find you've left something vital behind, something is broken, or not working properly. It instantly plays on your mind, hits your confidence, and once your confidence takes a tumble, your catches will too. Having full confidence in yourself and your equipment is as important as any other factor in being successful.

Some anglers like to carry a spare reel in case of a backlash on a multiplier reel during casting, or the loss of a lot of line. If you feel this important, then add a spare reel. It falls in to the confidence band and without a spare it may play on your mind and affect your concentration.

TACKLE BOX ORGANISATION

One quick glance inside an angler's tackle box tells me whether he's keen, or just along for a day out. Untidy tackle boxes strewn with forgotten rusted rigs, open packets of hooks and accessories, and other useless stuff that will never see the light of day are the norm in sea fishing. Lifting all this out to find items hidden underneath costs time and achieves nothing.

Tackle box organization is a vital element in fishing successfully and minimises lost time trying to find wanted items. Exactly how your box is organised is a personal thing that evolves over time to suit how and where you fish.

It doesn't matter whether you prefer a large box, rucksack, or other type of tackle bag. My prerequisite is that everything is immediately to hand and easily identified. I put shock leader material in to a padded wallet. I do this to avoid the leader getting nicked or scarred by anything sharp or abrasive in the box. I have a separate tube-shaped padded holder for hook length lines in various breaking strains; the lightest on the left, getting heavier towards the right. I can tell at a glance which spool of line I need.

I have a securely closing clear small plastic box that contains all the lead weights I will need for that single session. Also in the base of the box are two divided bait trays that clip on the outside of my box for easy access to bait while fishing. I have a set of weigh scales in a wallet. I will add either a flask or bottle of water, my camera, and maybe a little food. Nothing else goes in the base of the box, bar my reels.

The box deliberately has a top tray that can be lifted out. In this are the items I may need immediately and most often. I carry a small divided flat tackle box. In the various compartments are packets of links, swivels, bait clips, beads, rig swivels, a few spare plastic booms, neoprene tubing and telephone wire. My hooks are retained in their packets to minimize corrosion, but I divide the size 2 hooks and smaller in to one box section, and put the larger hooks in another, these all in logical order by size. Having the hooks inside their packets and in a closed plastic box further reduces the chances of salt spray and damp accessing the contents. You can see that I have everything I may need with me, but it's minimal and easy to locate.

The only other things I carry are a well-equipped rig wallet with appropriate rigs for the trip, a pair of long-nosed pliers, a honing stone, scissors and bait elastic. As I use items, I replace them exactly where they came from in my box. In this way, when fishing at night, I can locate items I need without thinking, minimising any lost time. As previously mentioned, I keep on top of replacing anything I use. It's an easy regime, and one that eliminates mistakes.

Learn to carry only what you need. Additional weight and clutter is tiring when walking long distances to marks.

I do the same with the area I'm fishing in. I use my rod rest as the figurehead. I place my seat box rear of the rest and slightly to one side, always the side the wind is blowing from so the wind is on my back. My bait is either in the seat box trays, or laid out inside the cool box. If I use a main light source as well as my headlamp, this goes behind me so that it illuminates all the fishing area, and the rod tips. If you place your lamp up on the shingle above you, or purposefully carry a shove-in monopod-type bar with a hook on it for the lamp to hang from, the added height will illuminate a far greater area for you. That said, I try to avoid using main camp lights when casting close, or when bass fishing, as I find added artificial light can scare fish working close inshore.

If you keep your fishing camp as tidy as your tackle box, then you'll never leave anything behind, nor lose anything.

DOUBLE PATTING

It's important to understand that, if you fish just one rod, then you retrieve a rig with washed-out bait, then re-bait the rig and re-cast, this soaks up a good two to three minutes before you're ready to re-cast and be back fishing again. Let's analyse this further. You get no bites, so after 15 minutes or so, you wind in. If you're fishing a three-hook rig, you need to pull all the old bait off the hook. Now re-bait each hook and whip the bait with elastic thread. Maybe put the hooks in the bait clips if you're using clips, reset the wires on the grip lead, and only then are you ready to re-cast. This baiting-up procedure could take two to three minutes in total. If you make four casts every hour, that's 12 minutes of fishing time with bait in the water lost. If you are fishing two rods, then that lost time doubles to 24 minutes lost. If you also have a fish or multiple fish on and need to unhook them, then you can add another 30 seconds or more for each fish. Over the average five-hour fishing session, wasted time adds up to two hours or more. If you fish once a week, over a month it's eight hours. This is all dead, unproductive time. We need to reduce this lost time to a more acceptable minimum.

Double-patting is the use of ready-baited rigs that can be hung on your rod rest until needed to replace the original fishing rigs as you retrieve them for re-baiting. If you tie a clip link on to your shock leader, and make every rig with an open-eyed swivel or upside-down clip link, then as you retrieve the washed out rig, unclip it and clip on a freshly baited trace and cast out. The time loss is now just a few seconds. The time to re-bait and check over the just-retrieved rig, and unhook fish, is when the freshly baited rig has been cast out and is already fishing. This would normally be idle time, but by double-patting we are using dead time productively and keeping baits in the water for the maximum amount of time, thus giving ourselves the very best chance of catching fish.

Some anglers also have hook lengths rigged with lightweight clips at one end that can be clipped on and off rig swivels. This is another quick change option. Not necessarily for changing to a fresh bait, but a few of these are handy to have in your wallet in case you need to change a damaged hook length or hook.

The use of two rods is another basic form of double-patting. It means that at all times you have at least one set of bait or baits in the water fishing. By doing this, you keep some scent in the water to keep nearby fish interested and hunting, plus you are much less likely to miss any short period of fish activity, such as a shoal of coalfish passing through the surf, or single fish such as a bigger cod or bass passing by.

I also utilise this 'spare' time to prepare any baits, such as cut mackerel strips or pared-down squid slivers, or to open any fresh shellfish baits I may happen to be using. I also have crabs peeled and cut to size ready for re-baiting with so I just have to pick them up and put them on the hook. This again saves a few seconds in time that would otherwise be wasted. I only prepare three or four baits at a time, though, as I do not want them to dry out, either through sunlight or air contact.

I also see anglers put their rod rest and rods on the edge of the tide line, but put their box and bait 30 yards or more back up the beach, which is a breathing space ready for the tide coming in. But then each time they need to re-bait they make the long trek between rod rest and box, and back again. It saves a huge amount of time if you fix a plastic bait box with a tied-on lid to your rod rest with a screw fixing, so that you can have enough bait for a few casts immediately to hand. It's the simple things that make the difference.

Analyse your fishing over a period of time and see if there are any other ways you can save time and be more efficient when fishing. I guarantee there will be. Also take note, again over a period of time, of your catches as you make improvements to your time management. I guarantee that, overall, your catches will improve significantly.

Chapter 16:
Final Thoughts

In writing this book, I'm looking back at lessons I've learned over more than five decades of sea fishing. I learnt the hard way, step by step, mistake by mistake. I wanted to stick rigidly to looking at tactics that will increase your catch rate, improve your efficiency when fishing, and above all, give you a short cut to better catches.

There was no point in me adding chapters on tackle. Tackle development and design, something I've worked directly in for over 25 years, is, like all technology, moving at a rapid pace as new materials and ideas come in to play. If I talk about today's tackle, by tomorrow, it is obsolete. I want the information in this book to never suffer that indignity of old age. Though fish gradually are evolving, even in 500 years' time, if there are beaches, rock ledges, piers and breakwaters with the topography described, then the information within these pages will remain totally accurate. Fish are fish and how they feed will never change. They are creatures of habit, and if you learn their thinking, they become predictable.

I would strongly urge you to keep that fishing diary. I have done since the age of 14, and it has proved invaluable. I record the exact venue and area I fished, period of time I fished, the sea state, tide height, flood or ebb tide, wind strength and direction, cloud cover, night or day, successful rigs, baits, and anything else that I feel is relevant on the day. My diary is hand-written, as I prefer it. However, some of the new computer and mobile phone app type fishing diaries, and those that allow searching for key words and information, can be very useful when compiling information on specific things over time. What technology will provide us with in the future is anyone's guess, but it can only get better and more informative.

As time passes, the diary, or other notes, will reveal patterns that indicate when and in what sea conditions, weather patterns and wind direction individual venues fish best, and for what species. Although I'm blessed with a good and reliable memory, I still frequently consult my diaries to collect and verify my thoughts. My diaries have contributed greatly to the fish I've caught over the years.

I also use my mobile phone to record notes on anything that I feel might be relevant later on. An example might be a high tide marker in line with some feature between high and low tide. The phone camera can also be used to record specific detail. This makes sure you never forget.

I would strongly encourage you to experiment with your fishing. When it comes to tactics, and rigs, keep changing, testing, and modifying. My advice would be to never fear failure. If you have an open mind and question and dissect why any failure occurred, it is from such experiences you learn. What I would say about experimentation is that it is best done when there are plenty of fish around and you are getting frequent bites. By comparing two rigs, or two different types of tactics, side by side, that one-versus-one comparison is invaluable and will highlight the advantages and disadvantages.

Observational skills are another asset, though I fear these you are born with. Learning them is less easy. Just little things like noticing a group of birds working can pinpoint shoals of baitfish or mackerel that, in turn, pull in bigger predators such as bass. The changing colour of water as it deepens, or surface water that changes from smooth to choppy, indicating some underwater feature, can change your luck on the day. Never be afraid, when the immediate fishing chores are done, to briefly watch the scene in front of you. A quote I've made a few times in my magazine articles is to 'note the normal, and explore the unusual', and it does pay to do so in this sense.

Observation also applies when fishing alongside other anglers. Always keep an eye on the people to your immediate left and right. If they start catching, try to decipher what they are doing differently, such as casting distance. A casual walk up to say "Hello" is usually well-received and you can get a glance at their bait and maybe rigs. If a good conversation flows and the person is communicative, politely ask why he's been doing so well. If you say you are learning, most good anglers will be only too pleased to pass on a few helpful tips. Such conversations prove invaluable. Sometimes the conversation will go beyond the mark you are fishing and you may learn much more than you originally anticipated.

I've made reference as to how much importance confidence in yourself and what you're doing plays in fishing success. There are many things that can knock your personal confidence. An often experienced scenario is, as you pass a fellow angler, you politely ask, "Any good?", and the response comes back, "Nah, mate, not had a bite. Been like it for days!" Never let such things settle in your mind and reduce your expectation. It's more than likely that this hapless fellow has little idea of what he's supposed to be doing, has second-rate bait, chosen the wrong rig, or, more to the point, might be in the wrong place fishing for a species that isn't even there. You have a duty to one person, and one person only: yourself. This is not selfish, just self-preservation and common sense. I've seen anglers doing everything right, but with no expectation of a catch, come up empty; while, a few yards away, another guy not fishing as well gets a few fish. You have to believe!

What can really throw your fishing is if you began fishing with a friend who does not share your growing enthusiasm. At the outset, you're just fishing and all is well. Then you yourself get more and more in to the angling, but your buddy does not progress with you, or at the same pace. Experience of this tells me that, if you want to succeed, then you need to be ruthless and spend more time fishing either on your own, or find someone of like mind that also wants to fish to the best of their ability. It's brutal, but honest. Only the individual can decide whether they have the strength and inclination to do this.

Some of you may feel that the way I approach my fishing is hard work. It is hard work, but then it's a lot of fun too. What could be better than visiting a mark, maybe for the very first time, picking out a feature to fish to, anticipating a target fish, choosing the right rig and bait, then making a good catch? Little compares to the feeling of catching fish, especially big fish, by your own initiative. Those of us that live for angling, and catching fish, still shake with excitement, the same as we did when we caught our very first fish decades ago. This is why we do it. It is not just a way of life, but life itself.

I hope this book proves to be a lifelong companion for you, and that its pages begin, and take you on, a lifelong journey of self-discovery as they have me. If this book helps only a handful of you to become true anglers, then it has achieved exactly what I wanted it to.

Mike Thrussell
October, 2016